The Films
of Judy Garland

ALSO BY JAMES L. NEIBAUR

*Clark Gable in the 1930s: The Films
That Made Him King of Hollywood* (2021)

The Jean Harlow Films (2019)

*The Hal Roach Comedy Shorts
of Thelma Todd, ZaSu Pitts and Patsy Kelly* (2019)

The Andy Clyde Columbia Comedies (2018)

The W.C. Fields Films (2017)

*Chaplin at Essanay:
A Film Artist in Transition, 1915–1916* (2008)

*Arbuckle and Keaton:
Their 14 Film Collaborations* (2007)

The Bob Hope Films (2005)

*The RKO Features:
A Complete Filmography of the Feature Films Released
or Produced by RKO Radio Pictures, 1929–1960*
(1994; paperback 2005)

BY JAMES L. NEIBAUR AND GARY SCHNEEBERGER

*Frank Sinatra on the Big Screen:
The Singer as Actor and Filmmaker* (2022)

BY JAMES L. NEIBAUR AND TED OKUDA

*The Jerry Lewis Films:
An Analytical Filmography of the Innovative Comic*
(1994; paperback 2013)

BY TED OKUDA AND JAMES L. NEIBAUR

*Stan Without Ollie:
The Stan Laurel Solo Films, 1917–1927* (2012)

ALL FROM MCFARLAND

The Films of Judy Garland

JAMES L. NEIBAUR

McFarland & Company, Inc., Publishers
Jefferson, North Carolina

All photographs are from the author's collection.

ISBN (print) 978-1-4766-8595-3
ISBN (ebook) 978-1-4766-4702-9

LIBRARY OF CONGRESS AND BRITISH LIBRARY
CATALOGUING DATA ARE AVAILABLE

Library of Congress Control Number 2022038599

© 2022 James L. Neibaur. All rights reserved

No part of this book may be reproduced or transmitted in any form or by any means, electronic or mechanical, including photocopying or recording, or by any information storage and retrieval system, without permission in writing from the publisher.

On the cover: publicity still of Judy Garland, 1945

Printed in the United States of America

*McFarland & Company, Inc., Publishers
Box 611, Jefferson, North Carolina 28640
www.mcfarlandpub.com*

For my grandnephew Rigel.

Acknowledgments

As always, first and foremost, my greatest thanks must go to my assistant Katie Carter, who lives every book with me, watching the films, offering her own ideas, checking my facts and fixing my typos. She remains invaluable.

Thanks to the late Mickey Rooney, who I interviewed when he appeared on stage at my old high school back in 2001. Mr. Rooney's personal memories of knowing and working with Judy Garland add a nice touch to this book about her films.

Thanks to the late Robert Osborne and Turner Classic Movies for their informative telecasts regarding Judy Garland's life and work, and for keeping her films alive and accessible to be enjoyed by future generations.

And thanks also to Terri Lynch, Kelly Parmelee, Ted Okuda, Gary Schneeberger, Peter Jackel, Phil Hall, and to the memory of my late wife Diana and late son Max, who continue to inspire everything I do.

Table of Contents

Acknowledgments   vi

Preface   1

The Early Years: From Frances Gumm to Judy Garland   3

Pigskin Parade   5

Every Sunday   10

Broadway Melody of 1938   13

Thoroughbreds Don't Cry   18

Everybody Sing   22

Love Finds Andy Hardy   26

Listen, Darling   30

The Wizard of Oz   33

Babes in Arms   48

Andy Hardy Meets Debutante   55

Strike Up the Band   58

Little Nellie Kelly   64

Ziegfeld Girl   69

Life Begins for Andy Hardy   76

Babes on Broadway   79

For Me and My Gal   83

Presenting Lily Mars   89

Girl Crazy   95

Meet Me in St. Louis   100

Table of Contents

The Clock 109
The Harvey Girls 116
The Pirate 123
Easter Parade 129
In the Good Old Summertime 137
Summer Stock 142

Back on Stage: 1951–1954 150
A Star Is Born 153

Returning to the Concert Stage 161
Judgment at Nuremberg 163
Gay Purr-ee 166
A Child Is Waiting 171
I Could Go on Singing 175

The Final Years 182

Chapter Notes 185
Bibliography 189
Index 191

Preface

Judy Garland is one of the true icons of classic Hollywood. This is due to a lot of great films, but perhaps mostly as a result of the timeless classic *The Wizard of Oz* (1939). Due to annual television showings from the 1950s onward, and later video releases and streaming opportunities, *The Wizard of Oz* is a film experience that even those with no interest in cinema's history are aware of and have embraced to the point of introducing it to ensuing generations.

It is also noted that Garland was a complex person who had a difficult, tumultuous life. But despite what might have been going on, or how unreliable she became, her performances in later dramatic films like *A Star Is Born* (1954) and *Judgment at Nuremberg* (1961) exhibited other aspects of her massive talent.

This book is a film-by-film look at Garland's motion picture work. It is not a biography. It will not attempt to explore her insecurities, impulses, or choices with any depth. They will be acknowledged, but only to the extent that they pertain to her work. This study will, however, examine Garland's humble cinematic beginnings, her rapid rise in popularity, and her versatility as an actress. It will discuss how she started out as a cute but plain stereotype and quickly emerged as a magnificent presence that defined every role she played.

So many studies have explored, analyzed, and judged Garland's life, but not enough give any real attention to her work. One of the greatest stars from the golden age of Hollywood cinema, Garland had a career that spanned from childhood to middle age, and that flourished by reinventing itself constantly despite offscreen demons. Her movie work certainly deserves to be discussed, assessed, appreciated, and celebrated. As impactful and significant as her bravura musical performances, the films of Judy Garland reveal a true artist with innate talent who was guided, cultivated, abused, and exploited to the point where every movie role she played demands at least some attention.

This film-by-film study will concentrate only on the movies in

Preface

which Garland had a significant role, even if it was a small supporting part. Films in which she made a guest appearance or a cameo as herself will be acknowledged in the text, but they will not merit full appraisal—these include *Thousands Cheer, Ziegfeld Follies, Till the Clouds Roll By, Words and Music, Pepe,* and the short subject *If I Forget You*. Discussion of these appearances will be merely transitional within the context of her filmography.

What this book will do is examine how her talents were gradually realized and understood, how opportunities presented themselves to help advance her career, how she responded to different co-stars and directors, and how she balanced her painful insecurities with her often focused and driven approach to her work. Her offscreen problems manifested themselves so strongly that they would sometimes affect her behavior on the set. But even those films that dealt with tardiness, sick days, and other obstacles from Garland's erratic behavior would offer exceptional performances on the screen. Eventually, these problems became too much for even the most patient filmmakers, and Garland's movie output became sporadic as she returned to live performances. But even during this period, she did not give up on movies altogether and would impress us with the occasional screen performance while her concert appearances were redefining her career.

Judy Garland's motion picture work is just one aspect of her amazing talent, but it is a part of her career that deserves closer examination. That is what this book will try to accomplish.

The Early Years
From Frances Gumm to Judy Garland

Judy Garland was born Frances Gumm in Grand Rapids, Minnesota, on June 10, 1922. The youngest of Frank and Ethel Gumm's children, she was nicknamed Baby by her family. Frank Gumm ran a movie theater and often had his talented daughters sing on stage before the movie. This continued when the family relocated to California in 1926, where the Gumm sisters expanded their appearances to the vaudeville circuit. With the urging of their mother, the girls even made some film appearances in very early talkies, including the Mayfair Pictures short film *The Big Review* (1929), as well as three Warner Brothers Vitaphone shorts, *A Holiday in Storyland*, and *The Wedding of Jack and Jill* (both 1930).

It was during a 1934 vaudeville tour when comedian George Jessel suggested that the Gumm Sisters change their name, noticing that audiences sometimes laughed when they were introduced. There are several stories as to how they ended up being billed as Garland. Some say Jessel came up with the name after seeing Carole Lombard play the character Lily Garland in the 1934 film *Twentieth Century*. Judy Garland's daughter, Lorna Luft, recalled that the name was inspired by Jessel calling the girls "prettier than a garland of flowers." Jessel himself, who lived until 1981, would frequently take credit for inspiring the name change, but would always tell conflicting stories as to how and where he came up with the name Garland. However mysterious her last name's creation might have been, Judy Garland remembered quite accurately that she chose the name Judy from a popular Hoagy Carmichael song by that title.

In the fall of 1935, Louis B. Mayer sent songwriter Burton Lane to the Orpheum Theater in Los Angeles to watch The Garland Sisters perform. Garland was selected for a screen test at Metro-Goldwyn-Mayer MGM, where she and her father showed up for an audition. She sang a Yiddish

The Gumm Sisters during their vaudeville days. Top row: Mary Jane and Dorothy Virginia Gumm. Bottom row: Frances Ethel (Judy Garland) Gumm.

standard, "Eli Eli," and the popular song "Zing! Went the Strings of My Heart." It turned out to be just an impromptu audition, and no screen test ended up being made.

Frankly, Garland really didn't have a lot going for her when she first showed up to audition. She was cute, not glamorously beautiful. She was

The Early Years—*Pigskin Parade* (1936)

only thirteen years old, which was too old to be a child star and too young to play adult roles. She was very short—under five feet tall.

However, Garland's talent when singing the songs exhibited an undeniable charisma that overshadowed any initial limitations, and the savvy MGM reps had no problem recognizing it. She was immediately hired, even though the studio really didn't know exactly what to do with her. Shortly after this triumph, Garland's personal life took a major hit when her father died in November 1935, leaving her heartbroken.

Mayer had also hired another girl singer around the same age named Deanna Durbin. He wasn't quite sure what the studio was going to do with two young female singers and wondered if he should let one of them go. While pondering this decision, Garland was loaned out to Fox Studios to play a small part in their football comedy *Pigskin Parade*. After completing her scenes for that project, she returned to her home studio and was shunted into a short subject playing opposite Deanna Durbin. The short, *Every Sunday*, was designed to contrast the two girls' singing styles—Durbin's being classically trained operatic and Garland's being vaudeville trained pop standards with a touch of swing. Upon screening the film, Mayer felt that both girls were so talented he didn't want to lose either. He told his staff to create a film in which they acted as a singing team.

Mayer was quite angry when he discovered that MGM wasn't quick enough to pick up Deanna Durbin's option and she had been hired away by Universal to star in the musical *Three Smart Girls* (1936), which became a huge hit and established Durbin as a star. As a result, MGM focused all of its attention on Garland. But it still wasn't quite sure exactly how to best showcase her.

As it turned out, Garland would stay with MGM for the next fifteen years and would never again be loaned out after that initial job at Fox to appear in *Pigskin Parade*, which is significant today as Judy Garland's feature film debut.

Pigskin Parade

Directed by David Butler
Screenplay by Harry Turgend, Jack Yellen, and William Conselman
   (based on a story by Arthur Sheekman, Nat Perrin, and Mark Kelly)

The Films of Judy Garland

Produced by Darryl F. Zanuck
Cinematography by Arthur C. Miller
Film editing by Irene Morra
Songs:
  "It's Love I'm After"; Lyrics by Sidney D. Mitchell; Music by Lew Pollack
  "You're Slightly Terrific"; Lyrics by Sidney D. Mitchell; Music by Lew Pollack
  "You Do the Darndest Things, Baby"; Lyrics by Sidney D. Mitchell; Music by Lew Pollack
  "The Balboa"; Lyrics by Sidney D. Mitchell; Music by Lew Pollack; Danced by Dixie Dunbar and cast
  "The Texas Tornado"; Lyrics by Sidney D. Mitchell; Music by Lew Pollack
  "Down with Everything"; Written by the Yacht Club Boys
  "Woo! Woo!"; Written by the Yacht Club Boys
  "We'd Rather Be in College"; Written by the Yacht Club Boys
  "Football Song"; Written by the Yacht Club Boys
  "We Brought the Texas Sunshine Here with Us"; Written by the Yacht Club Boys
Cast: Stuart Erwin, Patsy Kelly, Jack Haley, Johnny Downs, Betty Grable, Arline Judge, Dixie Dunbar, Judy Garland, Tony Martin, Fred Kohler, Jr., Grady Sutton, Elisha Cook, Jr., Edward J. Nugent, Julius Tannen, Emma Dunn, Jack Best, Edward LeSaint, George Offerman, Jr., Douglas Wood, Maurice Cass, Charles Croker-King, George Herbert, Eric Mayne, Cyril Ring, Hal Sieling, Lynn Bari, Ben Hall, Pat Flaherty, John Dillon, June Gale, George Harvey, Sam Hayes, Si Jenkis, Thomas Kellard, Al Klein, Orville Matthews Jack Matthews, Muriel Schenk, David Sharpe, Jack Stoney, Robert McLung, Alan Ladd, and the Yacht Club Boys
Released October 26, 1936
20th Century Fox
93 minutes
Black and White

Judy Garland had already filmed the musical short *Every Sunday* for MGM opposite Deanna Durbin, but it hadn't yet been released when 20th Century Fox asked for her to appear in a feature they were preparing. Having heard her sing and speak on a radio program sponsored by Chesterfield cigarettes, Fox asked MGM to loan her for the role of a hillbilly kid sister. Louis B. Mayer was away at the time, and the remaining

The Early Years—*Pigskin Parade* (1936)

executives in charge saw no problem with Garland being loaned out for the Fox feature, realizing that MGM would be receiving her compensation. This was around the same time that Deanna Durbin's option was not picked up quickly enough, allowing Joe Pasternak at Universal to cast her in *Three Smart Girls*. Mayer was quite angry that he not only lost Durbin, but his other new young girl was making her feature film debut at another studio before he was able to release the short that both girls appeared in together.

While going to a strange movie lot where she didn't know anyone was a bit daunting to the young newcomer, Garland was excited about appearing in her first feature film and playing a role that was comical and outrageous. While later studies have often been dismissive of the fact that she was a freckled, barefoot hillbilly stereotype in her first movie, Garland herself realized she could have fun and make some impact in the role, especially since she would be given the opportunity to sing.

The plot of *Pigskin Parade* has Yale University wanting to set up a benefit football game, but seeking a prestigious college whose football team is not particularly good. They choose the University of Texas, but an office worker accidentally invites the small-town Texas University that has a student population of only 700 and a ramshackle football team with only one true star. Texas U also just hired a new coach, Slug Winter (Jack Haley), who shows up at the college with wife Bessie (Patsy Kelly) with the intention of whipping the school team into shape. On his first day, he receives notice that Yale has invited the Texas U team for a game and accepts. Yale discovers its error but, in order to save face, decides to go through with it. They plan to fire the underling who made the error, but he promises to build up the opposing team in the press so everyone expects a good game. Meanwhile, Bessie comes up with the idea that because the lackluster football team is actually quite good at basketball, they could engage in rapid passing on the field as they do on the court to baffle the other team. However, when Bessie confiscates a bottle of gin from student Grady Sutton and drinks it herself, she drunkenly and clumsily causes the team's star quarterback Biff Bentley (Fred Kohler, Jr.) to break his leg. Bessie then discovers a hillbilly melon farmer, Amos Dodd (Stuart Erwin), tossing watermelons like footballs to his sister Sairy (Judy Garland), who catches them in a net. She quickly convinces them to come to the university and enroll. Amos's credentials are lifted from a smart but rebellious student (Elisha Cook, Jr.) who has been goaded into breaking a bank window in a protest against capitalism and is taken to jail. A blizzard hits Connecticut when

7

The Films of Judy Garland

Texas U travels there for the game, causing the warm-weather Texans to slip and slide in the snow. Amos, used to going barefoot, removes his shoes and socks, which gives him proper traction, and scores the winning touchdown.

Pigskin Parade is actually quite a delightful musical comedy that is light, amusing, and contains some fun songs and dances. Fresh-faced Johnny Downs and a young Betty Grable are a couple of popular students who earnestly support their school and are excited for the publicity a game against Yale can bring. Dixie Dunbar's singing and dancing and Tony Martin's singing are also part of the student body, whose musical rallies are a series of happy numbers. Arline Judge is the flirtatious girl who flirts with a number of different boys, including Amos, who is distracted enough by her aloofness toward him to temporarily make him want to return to the farm.

In her film debut, Judy Garland is filled with discernible energy as the rural Sairy, with a strong southern accent and an excitement for the opportunity afforded her and Amos. It is she who convinces her brother to go to college so that she can go, too. However, the film is not about Garland's character, who remains on the periphery of the narrative. Even when her brother wins the big game, and there are many cutaways to Downs, Grable, et al. watching from the stands, there are no shots of her reacting. However, Sairy does lead the victory parade and final song number that closes the movie.

There is an amusing running

Judy Garland's role was so small in her feature film debut that her name wasn't even mentioned in the newspaper ads for *Pigskin Parade*.

8

The Early Years—*Pigskin Parade* (1936)

gag where Sairy tells the others that she can sing, then asks, "Wanna hear me?", to which the others say, "Sure, later." When she finally does get to sing, it is the show-stopping number "It's Love I'm After," which is certainly the strongest musical number in the film. This gag was not particularly funny to audiences in 1936, who did not yet know Judy Garland, but for us watching it now and knowing her talent and all her success, it's very amusing to see her practically begging to sing and being dismissed.

In her small role, Garland manages to resonate enough with her winning personality, energetic performance, and wonderful singing voice to make some impact despite not being a major part of the movie's plotline. It is also historically interesting that, in her first film, Garland appears with Jack Haley, as both would make movie history in *The Wizard of Oz* a few years later.

For the remainder of her life, Garland would recall how kind Patsy Kelly was to her when she was intimidated by appearing in her first feature at a strange studio. Kelly kindly took Garland under her wing and calmed her nervousness. At the time, Kelly had just finished a strong series of short comedies opposite Thelma Todd at Hal Roach Studios, during which she had the opportunity to appear in features between two-reel assignments. She was especially amusing in support of Jean Harlow in *The Girl from Missouri* (1934). When she made *Pigskin Parade*, it was shortly after screen partner Thelma Todd was found dead under mysterious and tragic circumstances, and Hal Roach Studios were searching for another actress to play opposite her in the popular short films. But Kelly recalled when she first came over to the Thelma Todd series to replace ZaSu Pitts, and how intimidated she felt despite years of experience on stage. This caused her to connect with Garland, who would later tell Kelly, "You were the first one to be nice to me."[1] Incidentally, Stuart Erwin's bumpkin performance was so well received that he was nominated for an Oscar.

Pigskin Parade was filmed in August and September 1936 and ready for release in October. It was an enormous hit for the studio, and while Louis B. Mayer was happy that his actress made her feature debut before Joe Pasternak was able to finish and release Deanna Durbin's first movie *Three Smart Girls* (which came out a couple months later), he was quite angered that it was in a Fox picture and not one for MGM. The studio kept Garland busy appearing at various benefits and singing on the radio as an MGM player, and she was getting a great deal of attention for her talent. But the studio brass continued to search for just the right vehicle to show off her talents as a singer and actress, as well as her tireless charisma.

The Films of Judy Garland

Betty Grable, Emma Dunn, Judy Garland, Johnny Downs, and Dixie Dunbar in a scene that was cut from *Pigskin Parade*. Emma Dunn does not appear in the movie.

Fate stepped in when Garland was asked to do a novelty number at a benefit for Clark Gable, one of the studio's biggest stars. Gable had recently been named "The King of Hollywood," while another MGM star, Myrna Loy, was crowned queen. Garland sang a tribute to Gable that segued into the standard "You Made Me Love You." It was such a hit with the audience that Garland was assigned to perform the song again in her MGM feature film debut *Broadway Melody of 1938*. But first, the already produced *Every Sunday* hit theaters, because Mayer wanted his Deanna Durbin short out before her feature debut at Universal.

Every Sunday

Directed by Felix Feist
Screenplay by Mauri Grashin

The Early Years—*Every Sunday* (1936)

Produced by George Sidney
Cinematography by Charles Clarke
Songs:
    "Americana"; Written by Roger Edens
    "Il Bacio"; Music by Luigi Arditi; Lyrics by Gottardo Aldighieri
    "Waltz with a Swing"; Written by Con Conrad
Cast: Judy Garland, Deanna Durbin, Paul Irving, Thomas Pogue,
    Wright Kramer, Richard Powell, Tammany Young, Clem Bevans,
    Jack Lindquist, Kathryn Sheldon, and Jules Cowles
Released November 28, 1936
Metro-Goldwyn-Mayer
11 minutes
Black and White

Despite Mayer getting this one-reel short released before *Three Smart Girls* hit theaters, it was still making the rounds after the Deanna Durbin feature and generated some notice. As the film was a late 1936 release, theaters that didn't get around to playing *Every Sunday* until 1937 capitalized on the fact that new star Deanna Durbin was in the movie and Garland wasn't mentioned in the newspaper ads at all.

As stated previously, *Every Sunday* was made with Judy Garland and Deanna Durbin to determine which young lady should be signed to an MGM contract, and Mayer was pleased with both, but while he was away Joe Pasternak snatched up Durbin to star in the Universal feature *Three Smart Girls*. This is actually the most likely story out of many that have appeared in various studies. For instance, some claim Durbin was the choice, but a clerical error

When the MGM one reel short *Every Sunday* was finally released, Deanna Durbin had become a breakout star with Universal's *Three Smart Girls*. Thus, she got the attention in the newspaper ads.

hired Garland instead. There is even the offensive claim that an angry Mayer stated, "We'll make an even bigger star out of the fat one!" As late as 2002, director George Sidney, then in charge of screen tests, stated that casting director Billy Grady mistakenly hired Garland rather than Durbin.

Perhaps the most intriguing claim is that Deanna Durbin and Judy Garland performed together in a short film before this one that was available only to exhibitors, but that film has since been lost. However, it made enough of an impact that MGM produced a new short to be available to the public, hence *Every Sunday*. Why couldn't they simply give the movie made for exhibitors a wide release? Finally, there are even claims that Joe Pasternak had originally intended the role in *Three Smart Girls* to be for Garland, but when she was hired by MGM and Durbin was not, he chose the other girl.

Whatever the case, Durbin went to Universal, Garland stayed at MGM, and Mayer managed to get this short released before Pasternak's feature, thus having Deanna Durbin appear in an MGM film before her feature at Universal. Studio records indicate that Durbin and Garland recorded their songs on June 30, 1936. This is around two months before Garland went to Fox to start work on *Pigskin Parade*.

The basic plot for *Every Sunday* has Edna's (Deanna Durbin) grandfather leading an orchestra that plays in the town's park every Sunday. The city council threatens to replace the old man's orchestra, so Edna gets her friend Judy (Judy Garland) to join her, and they sing at the next park concert to generate interest. To contrast the two girls, Edna sings the aria "Il Bacio" and Judy sings Americana.

It's interesting to consider this film as either an additional audition or a competition between the two girls. Garland shines way more than Durbin in this film. Durbin sings beautifully, but she seems a bit stilted, not to mention the fact that in the opening scenes Garland's character appears much more proactive in their fight to save the job of Durbin's grandfather. Garland has a lot more of a presence when she performs, too—maybe it's just the nature of the more upbeat pop music she excelled at versus Durbin's arias, but Garland is much more memorable here. The girls play off each other well in the final song when they perform together.

MGM hired Judy Garland and lost Deanna Durbin, but it was Durbin who was a new box office hit when *Every Sunday* was making its rounds in theaters due to her starring film being released before Garland was able to make an impact. Of course, this would all change

The Early Years—*Broadway Melody of 1938* (1937)

when a small part in her first MGM feature would create more attention for Garland than for any of the leading players in *Broadway Melody of 1938*.

Broadway Melody of 1938

Directed by Roy Del Ruth
Screenplay by Jack McGowan (based on a story by McGowan and Sid Silvers)
Produced by Jack Cummings
Cinematography by William H. Daniels
Film editing by Blanche Sewell
Songs:
    "Broadway Melody"; Music by Nacio Herb Brown; Lyrics by Arthur Freed
    "You Are My Lucky Star"; Music by Nacio Herb Brown; Lyrics by Arthur Freed
    "Yours and Mine"; Music by Nacio Herb Brown; Lyrics by Arthur Freed
    "The Toreador Song"; from *Carmen;* Music by Georges Bizet; Libretto by Henri Meilhac and Ludovic Halévy
    "Follow in My Footsteps"; Music by Nacio Herb Brown; Lyrics by Arthur Freed
    "Everybody Sing"; Music by Nacio Herb Brown; Lyrics by Arthur Freed
    "Some of These Days"; Music and Lyrics by Shelton Brooks
    "I'm Feelin' Like a Million"; Music by Nacio Herb Brown; Lyrics by Arthur Freed
    "Largo al factotum"; from *Il Barbiere di Siviglia* (The Barber of Seville); Music by Gioachino Rossini; Libretto by Cesare Sterbini
    "You Made Me Love You I Didn't Want to Do It"; Music by James V. Monaco; Lyrics by Joseph McCarthy; Additional lyrics "Dear Mr. Gable" by Roger Edens
    "Your Broadway and My Broadway"; Music by Nacio Herb Brown; Lyrics by Arthur Freed
    "Broadway Rhythm"; Music by Nacio Herb Brown; Lyrics by Arthur Freed

The Films of Judy Garland

"Got a Pair of New Shoes"; Music by Nacio Herb Brown; Lyrics by Arthur Freed

"Happy Days Are Here Again"; Music by Milton Ager; Lyrics by Jack Yellen

Cast: Robert Taylor, Eleanor Powell, George Murphy, Binnie Barnes, Buddy Ebsen, Sophie Tucker, Judy Garland, Charles Igor Gorin, Billy Gilbert, Raymond Walburn, Robert Benchley, Willie Howard, Charley Grapewin, Robert Wildhack, Barnett Parker, Helen Troy, King Baggot, Matt McHugh, Leo White, Charles Coleman, Dudley Clements, Harry C. Bradley, Gino Corrado, William Worthington, Rosita Cronin, Helen Day, Edna Mae Jones, Carole Landis, Patsy Lee, Mildred Rehn, Marjorie Reynolds, Clarice Sherry, Eddie Borden, Harry Holman, Frank McGlynn, Sr., Maidel Turner, June Wilkins, Monica Bannister, Bonnie Bannon, Shep Houghton, Delos Jewkes, Wilbur Mack, Charles C. Wilson, Pat West, and Harrison Greene

Released August 20, 1937

Metro-Goldwyn-Mayer

110 minutes

Black and White

Judy Garland might have found it a fun and interesting challenge to play Sairy in *Pigskin Parade,* but she certainly didn't like the movie itself when she attended the premiere with her mother. She wanted to leave before it ended, but her mother thought that would be bad behavior. She thought she looked fat, awkward, and that the movie itself was silly. Compounding her sorrow was the fact that Deanna Durbin's big starring musical for Universal, *Three Smart Girls,* was one of the biggest hits of the year, and there was already publicity about her next film being an expensive musical with conductor Leopold Stokowski entitled *100 Men and a Girl.* Durbin was quite obviously going places, while Garland's only credit was an awkward appearance in a small role at Fox. While MGM was still searching for the right vehicle in which to star Garland, they felt a supporting role in one of their popular and prestigious *Broadway Melody* movies would suffice as her MGM feature debut.

Although her role is small, Judy Garland makes a real impact in *Broadway Melody of 1938,* her first feature appearance in an MGM movie. As stated earlier, Garland was a huge hit at a benefit for actor Clark Gable when she sang the standard "You Made Me Love You" with a new intro directed toward Gable. However, despite what has been reported in some other studies, that performance was not the reason

The Early Years—*Broadway Melody of 1938* (1937)

for Garland being cast in *Broadway Melody of 1938*. Plans to cast her were already in place by the time she performed for Clark Gable. All that changed is that the number she sang for Gable, complete with the tribute intro, was added to the movie because the studio believed it would have the same impact on moviegoers as it had on Gable. They were right.

Broadway Melody of 1938 was not so much a part of a series as it was a part of a pattern that MGM had been producing since

Garland's song to Clark Gable in *Broadway Melody of 1938* is the film's highlight.

the early days of talkies. Their 1929 sound feature *Broadway Melody* won the Academy Award for best picture. After that, every few years, another *Broadway Melody* was released. *Broadway Melody of 1936* had been a very big hit, so MGM used several players from that film, including Robert Taylor, Eleanor Powell, and Buddy Ebsen, for *Broadway Melody of 1938*.

Robert Taylor plays Steve Raleigh, who plans to produce a Broadway musical after lining up a backer (Raymond Walburn). He wants to cast newcomer Sally Lee (Eleanor Powell), but the backer's wife (Binnie Barnes) insists that Steve cast a well-known performer to ensure better box office. Sally has a farm background, and when she discovers that a horse she raised is now being auctioned off as a working animal, she bids for it at an auction and wins, but does not have the money. Steve fronts her the money, and when the horse wins a race, she is able to help finance the show and be cast in the lead. Judy Garland plays Betty Clayton, the daughter of stage mother and boarding house owner Alice Clayton (Sophie Tucker), a former stage star herself.

Garland has a comparatively small part, but an impactful one. The film centers more specifically on Eleanor Powell, her friendship with Sonny and Peter (George Murphy and Buddy Ebsen), whom she meets when stowing away on a train to keep an eye on how the horse is treated. It is there where she also meets Steve, and where he sees her talent when she does some impromptu dancing with Sonny and Peter. But as delightful as Powell, Ebsen, and Murphy are in their musical numbers, Garland manages to steal the film with her showstopping numbers. Sophie Tucker initially comes off as one of those annoying stage mother characters, but she becomes much more interesting when we discover that she was once a successful performer herself. Her bit in the film's big final number that pays tribute to her is actually quite moving.

Broadway Melody of 1938 also allows Garland to do some acting, as she plays a character different than Sairy in *Pigskin Parade*, different from the characters she would subsequently play, and different from who she actually was. Betty Clayton first appears in producer Steve Raleigh's office with stage mother Alice pursuing any opportunity for her talented daughter. Garland plays Betty as completely uninterested, distracted by the slightest stimuli, and more preoccupied with the lollipop she is enjoying than with her mother's platitudes about her natural talent. Alice had been a stage star of some notoriety many years before, and she sees her daughter Betty as an extension of the family's showbiz legacy. Betty proves herself by performing an exciting version of "Everybody Sing," which was written for this film by Nacio Herb Brown and Arthur Freed, and perfectly fit Garland's talents. While the previous numbers by the adult stars were pleasant and enjoyable, Garland's jazz-based pop number is louder, more aggressive, and more exhilarating. It is, up to that very moment, the best musical number she had performed on film. It would only be matched by a later number that wasn't originally supposed to be part of the film.

The way Betty is introduced in this movie—dressed in childish clothes and sucking on a lollipop, despite the fact that she was really too old for those things—encapsulates the way MGM thought of her at this time: an awkward teenager who was either too old or too young for them to really know what to do with. But, of course, she proves what a graceful and mature performer she is as soon as she starts singing.

Songwriters Brown and Freed were quite established as movie songwriters by this time, penning the enduring classics "Singin' in the Rain" and "You Were Meant for Me" for MGM's first big musical feature of the sound era, *The Hollywood Review of 1929*. Thus, when told to create a number for Garland to perform in *Broadway Melody of 1938*, it was not a terribly difficult task. Garland's audition films revealed her expansive talent, and the songwriters knew that the studio was trying

The Early Years—*Broadway Melody of 1938* (1937)

to showcase her abilities and eventually find the right property for her to star in. When distracted, somewhat belligerent Alice launches into "Everybody Sing" in *Broadway Melody of 1938*, it completely takes over the production. Moviegoers of the period were suitably impressed and waited for her next song

Of course, the other big musical number Judy Garland has in *Broadway Melody of 1938* is the one that really captures the audience the same way it impressed the crowd at Clark Gable's birthday celebration. Some studies claim that it reduced the tough actor to tears, and on Garland's next birthday she received a charm bracelet from Gable. "You Made Me Love You" was made popular back in 1913 by superstar Al Jolson and becomes something of a standard by the late 1930s. The number is beautifully mounted, with starry-eyed Betty singing to a photo of Gable after doing her "Dear Mr. Gable" intro written by lyricist Roger Edens.

One significant portion of the song is a spoken refrain that is not part of the song lyrics at all but is essentially dialogue for the movie. In her heartfelt enthusiasm for Gable, Betty does a spoken word section that states:

> Ah gee Mr Gable, I don't wanna bother ya. You've got a lot of girls to tell you the same thing. But I just had to tell you about the time I saw you in *It Happened One Night*. That was the first time I ever saw you. And I knew right then you were the nicest fella in the movies. I guess it's because you were so natural-like. Not like an actor but like any fella you'd meet at school or at a party. Then I saw you in a picture with Joan Crawford. I had to cry a little, because you couldn't have her. Not till the end of the picture anyway. Then I saw you in person going into the Coconut Grove and you almost knocked me over. You smiled at me. And I cried all the way home just because you smiled at me for being in the way. I'll never forget it Mr. Gable. You're my favorite actor.

It is the part of the song where Garland goes from singer to actor in the course of the number. Betty's youthful honesty, sincerity, and passion helps define a character that is comparatively small in the context of the film. Furthermore, this portrayal of a starstruck teenager is perfectly age appropriate for Garland at this point.

There are other musical numbers in which Garland appears, including a dance bit with Buddy Ebsen, making Mr. Ebsen one of the actors who danced on film with both Garland and with Shirley Temple. Co-star George Murphy was another.

Broadway Melody of 1938 was a hit for MGM, and brought a great deal of important attention to Judy Garland. As executives continued to search hard for just the right vehicle in which she could star, they kept her busy with other projects that continued to allow her to exhibit her talents as an actress and a singer.

Her next film, *Thoroughbreds Don't Cry*, was essentially a vehicle to spotlight another of the studio's up-and-coming stars, Mickey Rooney. But the movie is important for Judy Garland as well. Garland and Rooney had been friends for a couple of years, having met during their studies at the school they attended on the MGM lot. They had a lot in common and connected with each other, and their first film together showed they connected on screen as well. *Thoroughbreds Don't Cry* would be the first of ten movies they'd do together, and the only one in which Judy Garland is billed ahead of Mickey Rooney.

Thoroughbreds Don't Cry

Directed by Alfred E. Green
Screenplay by Eleanore Griffin, J. Walter Ruben, and Lawrence Hazard
Produced by Harry Rapf
Cinematography by Leonard Smith
Film editing by Elmo Veron
Song:
"Got a Pair of New Shoes"; Music by Nacio Herb Brown; Lyrics by Arthur Freed
Cast: Ronald Sinclair, Judy Garland, Mickey Rooney, C. Aubrey Smith, Sophie Tucker, Forrester Harvey, Charles D. Brown, Frankie Darro, Henry Kolker, Helen Troy, Elisha Cook, Jr., George Chandler, Douglas Wood, Bob Tansil, Edgar Norton, Louis Natheaux, Donald Kerr, Lionel Belmore, Marie Blake, James Flavin, Robert Homans, Ernie Alexander, Don Brodie, Chuck Hamilton, Harry Depp, Chester Clute, Edward Earle, Wilbur Mack, Jack Norton, Frank Whitbeck, Eddie Shubert, Charles Wilson, Cliff Nazarro, and Russ Powell
Released December 3, 1937
Metro Goldwyn Mayer
80 minutes
Black and White

The Early Years—*Thoroughbreds Don't Cry* (1937)

Mickey Rooney's movie career dates back to the silent era, when, as Joe Yule, Jr., he starred in a series of comedies based on the Mickey McGuire comics. His mother even had his name legally changed to Mickey McGuire. He was being billed as Rooney by the time he was hired at MGM and appeared in such films as *Manhattan Melodrama* (1934), playing Clark Gable as a boy. Rooney was cast in the drama *The Devil Is a Sissy* (1936) opposite two of MGM's biggest young stars, Jackie Cooper and Freddie Bartholomew. Cooper had been in Our Gang comedies and scored big in such films in *The Champ* (1932) and *Treasure Island* (1934), both opposite Wallace Beery. Bartholomew scored in the studio's adaption of Charles Dickens' *David Copperfield* (1935). And, yet, Rooney outshone both of them in *The Devil Is a Sissy*, easily stealing every scene and convincing MGM to focus on building him up as a star in his own right.

Freddie Bartholomew was scheduled to appear opposite Mickey Rooney and Judy Garland in *Thoroughbreds Don't Cry*, but after his success in *Captains Courageous* (released that June), Bartholomew's people argued that he should receive a better salary. During these negotiations, it was discovered that Freddie's entry into the throes of adolescence was causing his voice to change. So, Bartholomew was replaced in *Thoroughbreds Don't Cry* by Ronald Sinclair, who was newly signed to the studio. Sinclair was smaller, slighter, and New Zealand-born, so he fit comfortably into the role considered for British-born Freddie Bartholomew. Freddie was loaned to 20th Century–Fox and more appropriately cast in their screen version of Robert Louis Stevenson's *Kidnapped* (1938).

Ronald Sinclair is actually billed first in the credits. The opening credits present the three actors walking toward the camera, arm-in-arm, with Sinclair on the left, Garland in the middle, and Rooney on right, causing the billing to be shown in that order.

The plot of *Thoroughbreds Don't Cry* has Mickey Rooney as jockey Timmie Donavan, who is hired to ride the racehorse Pookah that is coming over from England with his owner, Roger Calverton (Ronald Sinclair) and his grandfather (C. Aubrey Smith). Judy Garland plays Cricket, whose aunt (Sophie Tucker) owns a boarding house for jockeys. Used to unrefined types like Timmie, Cricket is attracted to the effete Roger's better manners. Roger doesn't fit in well with the more rugged jockeys until he proves himself in a fistfight. Timmie's estranged father pretends he is dying and needs money for an operation in order to convince his jockey son to throw the race. Pookah's loss so upsets Roger's grandfather that he suffers a fatal heart attack. Roger is then forced to sell the horse to raise funds for a trip back to England. When Cricket tells Timmie about Roger's plight, the jockey goes to his father for money and discovers the illness he claimed was a ruse. He steals his father's wallet and gives the money to Roger, who puts Pookah in a big race with the intention of Timmie riding him. However, Timmie is banned from riding so Roger must ride Pookah, with Timmie's instructions.

While the story concentrates chiefly on Mickey Rooney's character with Ronald Sinclair in support, Garland's supporting role allowed her more screen time than her previous films to exhibit her ability as an actress. Being friends with Rooney, who was a powerhouse on screen, helped inspire her performance, and while Cricket is enamored with Roger, her feelings for Timmie are discernible. The two of them are conflicted and argumentative throughout, in a manner that shows their underlying, even begrudging, attraction to each other.

Exhibitors were generally pleased with *Thoroughbreds Don't Cry* and wrote in to the trades indicating that their patrons were impressed with the young stars:

> A program picture much better than the average. Will outgross some of the so-called specials. Mickey Rooney gives a fine performance, as do all the cast, including Judy Garland, Ronald Sinclair and Sophie Tucker.
>
> One of the best I've had in my theater. Sinclair looks very promising. Rooney without peer. Garland swell. Sophie Tucker plenty hot. All in all a fine picture that will make money and please customers. Great for juveniles, but the grownups also enjoyed it immensely.[2]

Thoroughbreds Don't Cry was still part of a sort of holding pattern in regard

Mickey Rooney and Judy Garland were both on the cusp of stardom when they appeared in *Thoroughbreds Don't Cry*, their first film together. However, Rooney was on the fast track, and Garland's advancement moved more slowly.

The Early Years—*Thoroughbreds Don't Cry* (1937)

to Judy Garland's career. MGM continued to search for the right vehicle for her to command, and wanted to place her in a film opposite younger people closer to her age to see how she responded to them. They saw how comfortably she fit into the proceedings, and especially noticed her chemistry with Mickey Rooney.

Judy Garland, however, was not particularly pleased with being cast in *Thoroughbreds Don't Cry*, despite the opportunity to work with her pal Rooney. Her character was added to the script after it had been written, and she felt that after being with the studio for a couple of years, she should be starring in films. Deanna Durbin's continued success at Universal in movies designed for her talents was yet another factor that was bothersome to Garland. It wasn't so much jealousy as an example of where she herself should be at her own (arguably better) studio.

It is notable that *Thoroughbreds Don't Cry* is not a musical, and thus Garland only sings one song that is not part of the production. Because this role, unlike her previous ones, wasn't inserted into the movie to allow Garland to sing every so often, it allows her to showcase even more of her acting ability, even though she is still very much a supporting cast member. She's still a little awkward and charmingly shy in her scenes opposite Sinclair, but there's a fire in her in her scenes with Rooney that we haven't seen from her yet that's exciting.

Judy Garland is reteamed with Sophie Tucker, with whom she appeared in *Broadway Melody of 1938*. Because they exhibited some chemistry in the earlier film, where Tucker got to sing a couple of her signature tunes, the studio wanted them to act together in a dramatic movie. MGM was considering grooming Tucker in similar matronly roles as had been played by one of their biggest stars, Marie Dressler, who had died a few years earlier. Sophie Tucker recalled in her autobiography:

> I didn't particularly like my part. It was a part any fifty-dollar character actress could do better than I. Producer Harry Rapf kept telling me, "Here's your chance to be another Marie Dressler!" I said to L.B. Mayer and to everyone on the lot, Judy, if carefully handled and groomed, will be the big MGM star in a few years.[3]

Mickey Rooney was being worked hard at this point in his career, *Thoroughbreds Don't Cry* being the sixth feature he acted in that year. He would appear in even more the following year. One of Rooney's 1937 films was *A Family Affair*, which was supposed to be a simple, low-budget production about the small-town Hardy Family for neighborhood theaters in the Midwest. It became a sensation, and a sequel was ordered featuring the same characters, but a new cast (other than Rooney). The second film, *You're Only Young Once* (1938), was an even bigger hit, so that cast—Rooney, Lewis Stone, Fay Holden, Cecilia Parker, and Ann Rutherford—was signed to a series of films that continued for years. Judy Garland would be a featured player in a handful of the Andy Hardy films.

However, for her next project, Judy Garland was given the chance to both act and sing, in a film that was designed to appeal to modern youth. Garland liked that she had a larger role to play in *Everybody Sing* and that her character was central to the narrative.

Everybody Sing

Directed by Edwin L. Marin
Screenplay by Florence Ryerson and Edgar Allen Woolf (adapted from their story)
Produced by Harry Rapf
Cinematography by Joseph Ruttenberg
Film editing by William S. Grey
Songs:
"Swing Mr. Mendelssohn"; Music by Bronislaw Kaper and Walter Jurmann; Lyrics by Gus Kahn
"The One I Love"; Music by Bronislaw Kaper and Walter Jurmann; Lyrics by Gus Kahn
"Cosi-Cosa"; Music by Bronislaw Kaper and Walter Jurmann; Lyrics by Ned Washington
"Down on Melody Farm"; Music by Bronislaw Kaper and Walter Jurmann; Lyrics by Gus Kahn
"Swing Low, Sweet Chariot"; Written by Wallis Willis; Arranged by Henry Thacker Burleigh
"Quainty, Dainty Me"; Music and lyrics by Harry Ruby as Ruby and Bert Kalmar as Kalmar
"The Show Must Go On"; Music by Bronislaw Kaper and Walter Jurmann; Lyrics by Gus Kahn
"Snooks Why?—Because!"; Music and lyrics by Harry Ruby as Ruby and Bert Kalmar as Kalmar

The Early Years—*Everybody Sing* (1938)

"Ever Since the World Began / Shall I Sing a Melody?" Music and lyrics by Roger Edens
Cast: Allan Jones, Judy Garland, Fanny Brice, Reginald Owen, Billie Burke, Reginald Gardiner, Lynne Carver, Helen Troy, Monty Woolley, Adia Kuznetzoff, Henry Armetta, Michelette Burani, Mary Forbes, Elise Cavanna, Andrew Tombes, Ann Bupp, Edgar Dearing, Jacques Vanaire, Marek Windheim, Bonnie Bannon, James Donlan, George Guhl, Alphonse Martell, and Ethan Laidlaw
Released February 4, 1938
Metro Goldwyn Mayer
91 minutes
Black and White

When doing a study of Judy Garland's filmography, some of the most interesting discoveries are movies that are little known. While these films are not at the level of *The Wizard of Oz, Meet Me in St. Louis*, or *A Star Is Born*, there is something fascinating and revealing in journeying down the bypaths of an iconic movie star's career.

Decidedly one of the least known of her early films, *Everybody Sing* has some significance due to Garland having more screen time and being of greater importance to the narrative than her other films up to this time. Her character is a bit of a rabble rouser, disrupting a staid music school with her jazzy ideas. While this character is appealing, *Everybody Sing* is rarely revived because it has become an unsettling viewing experience in the 21st century due to its use of blackface, an outmoded form of expression from the pre–Civil Rights era.

Judy Garland plays Judy Bellaire, who has trouble connecting at her school due to her promoting jazz based musical numbers, which results in her expulsion. Her home life is disruptive. Her father is a failed playwright (Reginald Owen), her mother is a flighty actress (Billie Burke), and her older sister Sylvia is beautiful but spoiled (Lynne Carver). The family has an amusing Russian maid named Olga (Fanny Brice) and a handsome cook with a strong singing voice named Ricky (Allan Jones), who is attracted to Sylvia. The family attempts to send troublesome Judy off to Europe, but she escapes the ship and tries out for a musical while disguised in blackface. Here Judy's penchant for jazz is impressive, and her talent so strong she gets a starring role in the show. Ricky arranges to make a recording of a song that expresses his love for Sylvia, but she is being placed by family into an arranged marriage. Judy's parents are aghast when they discover she's starring in a musical, but eventually everyone reconnects, including Ricky with Sylvia.

The Films of Judy Garland

Judy Garland and Allan Jones in *Everybody Sing*.

While *Everybody Sing* is not as well-known among Judy Garland's earlier films, it is still pivotal. She made a connection to audiences with her music in *Broadway Melody of 1938*, and showed her acting skills in *Thoroughbreds Don't Cry*, but in *Everybody Sing*, she has the opportunity to display both.

However, perhaps the most important element to Garland's

The Early Years—*Everybody Sing* (1938)

experience with *Everybody Sing* is a promotional tour she did, which allowed her to go on stage at big venues in major cities like Chicago and New York and connect with audiences as only she could. It was the first opportunity she had to perform to live audiences at this level, which would be an important aspect of her later career.

Unfortunately, despite Garland's seven-week promotional tour, *Everybody Sing* was a box office flop. But despite its lack of success at this level, it was still an important challenge for Garland as a singer and actress, because it gave her the opportunity to play drama, to play comedy, and to perform strong musical numbers. The enthusiasm and exuberance in her performance, at every level, would permeate her characters in subsequent films.

The fact that this film centers around a family of creative people who all have big personalities makes it a little overly chaotic at some points, but for the most part Garland still manages to hold her own. Besides this film being a turning point for Garland's career, it's also notable for featuring Fanny Brice in one of her few film roles, and the only time her popular Baby Snooks character was committed to the screen. Just seeing two legends like Brice and Garland interact is a real treat. But the blackface number is a problem—not only the fact that it is there, but that it is used as part of the plot for a white character to try to get ahead in her performing career, and almost certainly intended to be amusing to audiences at the time. In a more enlightened era, it sours the entire movie.

Garland had a great deal of insecurity, especially during this time in her career, and despite the promo tour quickly revealing her as one of the greatest live performers in her time, the fact that the working title of *Everybody Sing* was *The Ugly Duckling* (referring to the character Garland played) kept her from having the same confidence that her pal Mickey Rooney brashly embraced. Add to this the fact that Deanna Durbin was on her third starring vehicle at Universal, *Mad About Music*, which was another big hit, while Garland was still trying to establish herself.

In her review for the *Los Angeles Evening Citizen News*, Elizabeth Yeaman states that Judy Garland should already be considered for more grownup roles:

> *Everybody Sing*, a boisterous burlesque of a theatrical family, is the latest offering at Grauman's Chinese and Loew's State theaters. The film presents Judy Garland in a role that amounts to starring proportions and it returns Fanny Brice to the screen for the first time since her brief skit in *The Great Ziegfeld*.

The Films of Judy Garland

Judy is a talented youngster, and when she sings she has definite art in her phrasing and delivery of modern songs. But since her talent is definitely adult, the studio would do well to give her the roles and wardrobe of an adult and thus eliminate that feeling of incongruity that creeps into the appearance of a precocious youngster.[4]

Fortunately, at about this time, MGM was coming closer to finding what they felt was the right vehicle for Garland's significant set of talents. Some exploration and discussions needed to happen, but the old Frank Baum story, *The Wonderful Wizard of Oz*, looked like the right basis for a film that could be constructed as a Judy Garland vehicle. While these negotiations were going on, Garland was kept busy by being placed in one of Mickey Rooney's popular Andy Hardy movies. The studio execs knew of Rooney and Garland's friendship, and their camaraderie on screen had also been established. It seemed like a perfect movie for Garland to do while waiting for her own starring vehicle to be ready.

However, Garland was cast in *Love Finds Andy Hardy* as the overlooked plain girl, bubbling with personality, but whose presence is overshadowed by pretty Ann Rutherford, already established as Andy's girlfriend Polly Benedict, and beautiful newcomer Lana Turner. Turning in a typically good, effervescent performance, Garland once again felt like the ugly duckling.

Love Finds Andy Hardy

Directed by George B. Seitz
Screenplay by William Ludwig (from a story by Vivien R. Bretherton)
Gag consultant: Buster Keaton
Produced by Lou L. Ostrow and Carey Wilson
Cinematography by Lester White
Film editing by Ben Lewis
Songs:
    "In Between 1938"; Music and lyrics by Roger Edens
    "It Never Rains but What It Pours"; Music and lyrics by Mack Gordon and Harry Revel
    "Meet the Beat of My Heart"; Music and Lyrics by Mack Gordon and Harry Revel

The Early Years—*Love Finds Andy Hardy* (1938)

Cast: Mickey Rooney, Judy Garland, Lewis Stone, Fay Holden, Cecilia Parker, Lana Turner, Ann Rutherford, Mary Howard, Gene Reynolds, Don Castle, Betsy Ross Clarke, Marie Blake, George P. Breakston, Raymond Hatton, Jay Ward, Rand Brooks, Jules Cowles, George Noisom, and Erville Anderson
Released July 22, 1938
Metro Goldwyn Mayer
88 minutes
Black and White

Judy Garland was involved in a car accident just as production was about to begin on *Love Finds Andy Hardy*, suffering three broken ribs. Her character in the movie was almost written out of the script, but Garland the trooper was ready to return to work three weeks later and performed while her ribs were still healing. According to the press:

> Judy Garland, girl movie singer who suffered three broken ribs and bruises in an auto collision, was in good condition and resting comfortably today at Cedars of Lebanon hospital. The young actress was en route home from a movie set in a Metro-Goldwyn-Mayer studio car driven by a chauffeur at the time of the accident.[5]

Love Finds Andy Hardy is one of the most important films in the Hardy Family series. While the previous films were pleasant, low budget entertainment that earned a good profit, *Love Finds Andy Hardy* was an enormous hit, profiting over a million dollars at the box office, and further securing Mickey Rooney's status as a leading man, despite his youth and short stature. By the year's end, Rooney would be the number one star at the box office, and he would retain that position for years.

While arrangements were being made for Garland's first starring vehicle, she played Betsy Booth in *Love Finds Andy Hardy*, which showcased her talents perhaps better than any of her movies thus far. Her first appearance in the film, for instance, happens when the doorbell rings, Andy looks to the front door, and sees the face of Betsy Booth smiling admiringly through the window. This image of Garland, full of bright, wide-eyed wonder and enthusiasm, would define her character for a number of subsequent films.

The story has Andy Hardy planning to buy his first car, a real junker, for only $20. Andy has a knack for tinkering with cars, so the fact that the auto needs repairs is not a factor. He has enough for a $12 down payment and plans to raise the remaining $8 by December 23, so he'll have his car in time for his school's Christmas dance. Things hit a

Judy Garland plays Mickey Rooney's pal in *Love Finds Andy Hardy*.

snag when Andy discovers that his girlfriend Polly Benedict (Ann Rutherford) will be away visiting family over Christmas and unable to attend the dance. Andy finds a way to make some money when his friend Beezy agrees to give him $8 if Andy will take his girl Cynthia (Lana Turner) to the dance. Beezy will be out of town with his family, and he wants Andy to date Cynthia so that she won't be seeing other guys while he's gone. Garland's character, Betsy Booth, is a 13-year-old girl who is visiting her grandmother next door to the Hardy home. Betsy develops a crush on Andy, but must settle for being his supportive pal. Betsy is more mature and pragmatic than Andy, who bungles even his responsibility to keep pretty Cynthia preoccupied.

The relationship between Andy and Betsy is a new element that is introduced to the Hardy series with this film, while further exhibiting the discernible chemistry between Rooney and Garland. Betsy supports Andy's struggles with other girls, while Andy is so preoccupied that he doesn't fully realize how much Betsy is helping him. When the wealthy Betsy buys Andy a new radiator cap for his car, he talks about how much

The Early Years—*Love Finds Andy Hardy* (1938)

it will impress Cynthia. Andy doesn't realize he has hurt Betsy's feelings. Betsy lets out her emotions with the song "In-Between."

It's interesting that Garland was cast as a character who is 12 or 13 years old, when she in fact was a couple years older than that in real life. The main reason why Andy doesn't pay attention to her for much of the film is because he sees her as a child. The friendly relationship between Betsy and Andy is delightful, but it's as if the studio still did not see her as someone who could play a romantic part, even in a teen movie.

Complications arise when Polly returns early, in time to attend the dance, and Andy must tell her he has other plans, as he is monetarily committed to taking Cynthia. Then Beezy writes Andy and says he found another girl while visiting relatives and no longer wants Cynthia, so the deal is off. This leaves Andy without the money to buy his car; stuck dating Cynthia, who he finds pretentious; and unable to calm his actual girlfriend Polly, who is understandably upset. Betsy fixes things by telling Cynthia that Andy's car is a real junker, so the haughty girl refuses to go with him, delighting Andy considerably.

The way everything works out is perfectly typical of the Hardy Family movies. Mrs. Hardy is called out of town when her mother suffers a stroke. There is no way to reach her by conventional means, so Andy brings his father, Judge Hardy, to a friend who has a ham radio outfit, and arrangements are made for a message to be sent to Mrs. Hardy; subsequently, a response is returned to Andy and the judge. While crude technology in the 21st century, ham radio communication was quite innovative back in 1938 and impressed Judge Hardy, who earlier in the film recalled that he was well into adulthood when air flight happened. In its historical context, this aspect of the film is quite fascinating. In the context of the narrative, Judge Hardy is impressed enough to give Andy the $8 to pay for his car.

Andy's problems haven't quite ended, however. Polly is still angry about the situation with Cynthia. In fact, Andy discovers that despite the fact that he is now free, Polly has decided to go to the Christmas dance with a college boy. Saving the day yet again, Betsy comes over to the house wearing an evening gown, looking mature and beautiful, and offers to attend the dance with a dejected Andy, who brightens up considerably. The bandleader at the dance recognizes Betsy as the daughter of a famous singer and realizes she can also sing. She performs the songs "It Never Rains but What It Pours" and "Meet the Beat of My Heart" as only Judy Garland could, despite the pain of healing broken ribs.

Critics not only noticed that *Love Finds Andy Hardy* was superior to the other films in the series, they also pointed out Garland's contribution. The *Los Angeles Times* stated:

> In this new Hardy feature, Andy (Mickey Rooney) reaches the puppy love stage with a vengeance, gets into romantic complications with two winsome misses and is finally extricated by a third (Judy Garland) who comes to his rescue. Miss Garland, a new addition, gives a very fine performance, sings nicely and makes a fine foil for the effervescent Mickey.[6]

Love Finds Andy Hardy was an especially big movie for Mickey Rooney, whose salary went from $500 per week to $5000 per week. His next film, *Boys Town*, would be another major hit. However, Judy Garland was on the cusp of stardom with preparations already underway for *The Wizard of Oz*. In fact, Garland was already doing costume fittings for that production when the expansiveness of its intended scope caused a production delay. Rather than beginning filming in July 1938, plans were to start in October of that year. Continuing to keep busy, Garland began production on *Listen, Darling* opposite Freddie Bartholomew in June 1938. The production would complete in time for her to begin filming *The Wizard of Oz* in October.

Listen, Darling

Directed by Edwin L. Marin
Screenplay by Elaine Ryan and Anne Morrison Chapin (from a story by Katherine Bush)
Produced by Jack Cummings
Cinematography by Charles Lawton, Jr.
Film editing by Blanche Sewell
Songs:
  "Zing! Went the Strings of My Heart"; Music and lyrics by James F. Hanley
  "On the Bumpy Road to Love"; Music and lyrics by Al Hoffman, Al Lewis, and Murray Mencher
  "Ten Pins in the Sky"; Music and lyrics by Joseph McCarthy and Milton Ager
Cast: Judy Garland, Freddie Bartholomew, Mary Astor, Walter Pidgeon, Alan Hale, Scotty Beckett, Barnett Parker, Gene Lockhart, Charley Grapewin, and Edgar Dearing

The Early Years—*Listen, Darling* (1938)

Released October 21, 1938
Metro Goldwyn Mayer
75 minutes
Black and White

While preparations continued to be made for the production of *The Wizard of Oz*, MGM kept Judy Garland busy by placing her in this lighthearted B movie, for which she received top billing for the first time. She was cast (for the first and only time) opposite Freddie Bartholomew, whose career as a child star peaked and who was now exploring where he could go with his career as an adolescent.

The story is simple. Garland is Pinkie Wingate, a young girl whose mother Dottie (Mary Astor) has been widowed and finds herself unprepared to run things. She comes from a time when young girls were taught to cook and sew and little else. She wants better for her daughter. Because she needs the money to send Pinkie to a good school where her strong singing voice will be cultivated, Dottie is ready to marry Arthur Drubbs, who is enamored with her. Pinkie, however, realizes her mother truly doesn't love Drubbs. So, she and her pal Buzz (Freddie Bartholomew) trick Dottie and Pinkie's little brother Billie (Scotty Beckett) into boarding a trailer, and they hurriedly drive them out into the country to just get away from responsibility. It is out that there she meets Richard, a handsome photographer (Walter Pidgeon), and wealthy, affable J.J. Slattery (Alan Hale). Pinkie likes Richard, while Buzz prefers Slattery.

Listen, Darling had been in preparation for a year before being chosen as a vehicle for keeping Garland busy until *The Wizard of Oz* was ready for filming. The fact that she gets billing above established stars Mary Astor and Walter Pidgeon shows how MGM was ready to fully promote her to starring vehicles. But the studio was counting on *The Wizard of Oz* to be the movie that would fully establish Garland as a star. This was especially concerning when *Listen, Darling*, despite being on a low budget and running only 75 minutes (making it prime for double features), was a box office flop.

Even though she receives top billing, Garland seems to be more in a supporting role. Freddie Bartholomew gets the bulk of the focus and most of the scenes, as he is really the one orchestrating the whole scheme to find a suitable man for Dottie to marry. It's fun to see Mary Astor playing Garland's mother years before they played mother/daughter in the more famous *Meet Me in St. Louis*.

Judy Garland, Mary Astor, Walter Pidgeon, Scottie Beckett, and Freddie Bartholomew in *Listen, Darling.*

Garland sings only three songs in *Listen, Darling*, but one of them is "Zing! Went the Strings of My Heart," which was the song that she performed for Louis B. Mayer at her first audition, and which would become one of her signature tunes. Rather than her usual jazzy rendition of the song, in *Listen, Darling* she sings it as a ballad, and most

The Early Years—*The Wizard of Oz* (1939)

effectively. Reportedly, both versions were filmed and the ballad version was determined to be the strongest.

Freddie Bartholomew fell mightily hard for his co-star, sending flowers to Garland and pinning love notes on her dressing room door. She only considered Bartholomew a good friend and had no feelings for him beyond that.

Garland had no problem relating to the plot line of *Listen, Darling*, where a widowed mother was interested in marrying what her children perceived to be the wrong man. Garland's actual mother Ethel Gumm had planned to marry Will Gilmore, a man Garland did not like, and ended up doing so on the anniversary of her own father's death. Garland would later state, "That was the most awful thing that ever happened to me in my life. My mother marrying that awful man the same day my daddy died."[7]

Listen, Darling is short and breezy, but ultimately of little note to Garland's overall filmography. And despite its failure at the box office, exhibitors were pleased with this offering, with Ralph Talbot of the Majestic Theater in Tulsa, Oklahoma, stating:

> A picture that is not an epic, does not decide any world issues, is not a gigantic spectacle—BUT—for an hour and a half of rattling good entertainment, we recommend *Listen, Darling*. It was wholesome, fun, a dash of romance, some swell songs by Judy Garland, and a sparkling performance by an exceptionally capable cast. For a real treat, see *Listen, Darling*.[8]

However, while acknowledging Garland's songs, most of the critical reviews of *Listen, Darling* gave most of their attention to Freddie Bartholomew's performance.

Given less attention than her co-star, despite receiving top billing in this B movie, Garland was about to reach major stardom with her next film. *The Wizard of Oz* would define Garland's career, and would be so strong that it would command relentless popularity from the time of its initial release until well into the 21st century.

The Wizard of Oz

Directed by Victor Fleming, with contributions by George Cukor, Mervyn LeRoy, Norman Taurog, Richard Thorpe, and King Vidor

The Films of Judy Garland

Screenplay by Noel Langley, Florence Ryerson, and Edgar Allan Woolf (from the book by L. Frank Baum, adapted by Langley, and with contributions from Arthur Freed, Irving Brecher, William H. Cannon, Herbert Fields, Jack Haley, E.Y. Harburg, Samuel Hoffenstein, Bert Lahr, John Lee Mahin, Herman J. Mankiewicz, Jack Mintz, Ogden Nash, Robert Pirosh, George Seaton, and Sid Silvers)
Produced by Mervyn LeRoy with Arthur Reed
Cinematography by Harold Rosson
Film editing by Blanche Sewell
Songs:
- "Over the Rainbow"; Lyrics by E.Y. Harburg; Music by Harold Arlen
- Munchkinland Medley: "Come Out, Come Out, Wherever You Are," "The House Began to Pitch," "As Mayor of the Munchkin City," "As Coroner, I Must Aver," "Ding Dong the Witch is Dead," "Lullaby League," "Lollipop Guild," and "We Welcome You to Munchkinland"; Lyrics by E.Y. Harburg; Music by Harold Arlen
- "Follow the Yellow Brick Road"; Lyrics by E.Y. Harburg; Music by Harold Arlen
- "If I Only Had a Brain"; Lyrics by E.Y. Harburg; Music by Harold Arlen
- "We're Off to See the Wizard"; Lyrics by E.Y. Harburg; Music by Harold Arlen
- "If I Only Had a Heart"; Lyrics by E.Y. Harburg; Music by Harold Arlen
- "The Merry Old Land of Oz"; Lyrics by E.Y. Harburg; Music by Harold Arlen
- "If I Were King of the Forest"; Lyrics by E.Y. Harburg; Music by Harold Arlen

Cast: Judy Garland, Frank Morgan, Ray Bolger, Bert Lahr, Jack Haley, Margaret Hamilton, Billie Burke, Charley Grapewin, Clara Blandick, Pat Walshe, Billy Bletcher, Dorothy Barrett, Angelo Rossitto, Amelia Batchelor, Lorraine Bridges, Tyler Brooke, Candy Candido, Tommy Cottonaro, Jerry Maren, Jon Dodson, Harry Earles, Jackie Gerlich, Budd Linn, Abe Dinovitch, Phil Harron, Shep Houghton, Charles Irwin, Lois January, Ethelreda Leopold, Dona Massin, Eleanor Keaton, Nita Krebs, Yvonne Moray, Ambrose Schindler, Helen Seamon, Margaret Pelligrini, Rolfe Sedan, Elvida Rizzo, Oliver Smith, Katharine Snell, Robert St. Angelo, Robert Sudam, Harry Wilson, Buster Brodie, Harry Cogg, Sid Dawson, Sig Frohlich, Lee Murray, Jack

The Early Years—*The Wizard of Oz* (1939)

Paul, Betty Ann Cain, Franz and Josefine Balluck, Mickey Carroll, Eddie and Lida Buresh, Charles Becker, Nona Cooper, Freda Betsky, Ken Darby, Lewis Croft, Daisy Earles, Ethel and Prince Denis, Ruth Duccini, Ardith Dondanville, Gracie and Tiny Doll, Fern Formica, Jeanne La Barbera, Emil Kranzler, Joseph Herbst, Dolly Kramer, James R. Hulse, George Ministeri, Joan Kenmore, Elaine Merk, Valerie Lee, Karchy Kosiczky, Johnny Leal, Rae-Nell Laskey, Rad Robinson, William H. O'Docharty, Garland Slatten, Meinhardt Raabe, Parnell St. Aubin, Little Billy Rhodes, Ruth Smith, Garland Slatten, Alta Stevens, Gladys Wolff, Marie Winters, August Swenson, Betty Tanner, Gus Wayne, Victor Wetter, Johnny and Marie Winters, and Murray Wood

Released August 25, 1939
Metro Goldwyn Mayer
102 minutes
Sepia Tone/Color

A chapter on a film like *The Wizard of Oz* is somewhat daunting for any writer, in that it is not only a film that has lived on as a classic—it is an iconic motion picture that defined the career of everyone in it, and for many it represents the entire decade of 1930s cinema. There are people whose only film experience featuring a movie from before their lifetime is a screening of *The Wizard of Oz*.

MGM's intent on finding the right property for Judy Garland was certainly a sound one. Even they could not realize what an enormous and lasting impact *The Wizard of Oz* would make on her career, and on American

Judy Garland as Dorothy in *The Wizard of Oz*, which is perhaps her most iconic role.

cinema. It is even among the key reasons why many believe 1939 to be the greatest year in motion picture history.

There are studies that claim Shirley Temple was actually the first choice for the role of Dorothy, and that Garland was only chosen for the role after Temple's studio, 20th Century–Fox, refused to loan her for the production. This is partially true, but not completely accurate.

Samuel Goldwyn had acquired the movie rights to the L. Frank Baum Oz stories after Walt Disney enjoyed success with his full-length animated feature *Snow White and the Seven Dwarfs* (1937). The idea that an animated cartoon could successfully maintain feature length, let alone become a major hit movie, was considered a rather outrageous idea at the time. When Disney's film indeed became a major hit, other studios took notice and considered their own animated features or films based on children's books. Fleischer Studios, for instance, responded with their animated version of *Gulliver's Travels* (1938). Goldwyn bought the movie rights to the Baum stories, but hadn't pursued any sort of production when Twentieth Century–Fox contacted him in an attempt to buy the rights. It wanted to film *The Wizard of Oz* as a live action feature for Shirley Temple. A story in the *Los Angeles Times* reported:

> While Samuel Goldwyn has long considered producing *Wizard of Oz* as a picture, he may eventually relinquish the rights to this fantasy written by Frank Baum. Understanding is that Goldwyn has had no fewer than five large offers in the past week for the subject, because producers deem the film a follow-up for *Snow White and the Seven Dwarfs*. Right out in front among the bidders is Twentieth Century–Fox, which has intentions of presenting Shirley Temple as Dorothy. And wouldn't it be an idea if Jane Withers were also cast in the film?[9]

When Twentieth Century–Fox and Goldwyn didn't

Many wanted Shirley Temple to play the role of Dorothy.

The Early Years—*The Wizard of Oz* (1939)

come to terms, the studio made plans to instead star Shirley in *The Little Princess*.

Only days after the article on Fox's interest in the property, this item appeared in Louella Parsons' popular syndicated column:

> Remember Dorothy, the wizard, the Nome King and Belinda, the amazing hen from Frank Baum's childhood classics, the *Oz* books? Well, all these beloved characters are coming to the screen in Metro-Goldwyn-Mayer's production of *The Wizard of Oz* with Judy Garland already cast in the role of Dorothy. Probably it's the Snow White influence that is responsible for MGM's plans to bring another child's story to the screen and it is lucky to have prevailed upon Goldwyn to part with the screen rights. Sam has had many offers for the Baum stories, which he has held for years, but since he has no juvenile stars on his roster, he consented to part with them.[10]

Judy Garland was already doing costume fittings and other pre-production activities for *The Wizard of Oz* while filming *Listen, Darling*, but there were financial backers with the studio that argued for a bigger name in the role of Dorothy. They didn't particularly care that this project was chosen specifically for the talents of Judy Garland, whose work as a singer and actress had been cultivated over a series of movie appearances for the past two years. Their only perspective was that while Judy was an appealing performer, most of her movies flopped unless they were essentially carried by another performer (e.g., Mickey Rooney). They were in favor of borrowing Shirley Temple from Fox for the role. To keep its New York branch happy, MGM inquired as to the availability of Shirley Temple for *The Wizard of Oz*, but the studio refused to loan her out. Temple was already active on *The Little Princess*, which would be a box office hit, followed by another, *Susannah of the Mounties*, before her career went into a slump.

The Wizard of Oz had been filmed before, via several short films that date back to 1908 that presented one aspect or another from Baum's original stories. The only other feature-length version of the story was a rather notorious one by comedian Larry Semon in 1925. At the time, Semon was a wildly popular comedian whose movies were among the most successful at the box office. However, his quirky ideas and penchant for bigger-means-better gags worked better in short films than in features. His approach to *The Wizard of Oz* was typically surreal and today is a real curio.

Larry Semon's film does retain a character from the Baum books that does not appear in the 1939 film—King Krewl, known as Prime Minister Kruel in the Semon movie—and uses the name Pastora to

The Films of Judy Garland

Larry Semon, Dorothy Dwan, and Oliver Hardy in the 1925 silent version of *The Wizard of Oz*.

identify Princess Dorothy's father, as found in Baum's 1904 book *The Marvelous Land of Oz*. However, for the most part, Semon's movie is a real departure from the original source material, presenting Dorothy as 18 years old, not a child; making the Tin Man a villain who turns on the others; and focusing on the exploits of the Scarecrow. The Scarecrow, Tin Man, and Cowardly Lion aren't characters found in the land of Oz; rather, they are the farm hands who hide behind these disguises upon being whisked there with Dorothy after a cyclone. Semon cast his 19-year-old wife as Dorothy, Oliver Hardy (later of Laurel and Hardy fame) as the Tin Man, himself as the Scarecrow, and black comedian Curtis McHenry[11] as a stereotypical cowardly lion.

Because of comparison to the 1939 classic, the 1925 feature is often dismissed as an artistic and commercial failure. In fact, the film got good reviews in the trades upon being released, and also enjoyed some positive attention in the press. Even critics who admitted to the film's (and Larry Semon's) excesses believed it was overall a good family film with plenty of laughs and imagination, and it was recommended for parents to take their children to see it. However, the studio for which it was made, Chadwick, was already having financial troubles before Semon ignored budget restrictions with this lavish feature, and went bankrupt not long after production completed. Thus, distribution was so limited it played only in the bigger cities and didn't make back near its costs. Semon, who was financially active in the film's production, never recovered from this failure, causing him to have a nervous breakdown and likely contributing to his death three stressful years later.

Newspaper accounts continued to announce various cast members who were hired to appear in MGM's *The Wizard of Oz*. This included Ray Bolger as the Scarecrow, Bert Lahr as the Cowardly Lion, and Buddy Ebsen as the Tin Man. MGM wanted W.C. Fields to play the Wizard. Fields had just left his longtime studio of Paramount after poor health kept him off the screen for a year. According to the book *The W.C. Fields Films*:

> He was pleased with the opportunity, having been a fan of the L. Frank Baum stories.... An enthusiastic Fields began making notes as to how he would approach the character, and was planning to call a meeting with MGM representatives about the project. However, Fields also realized this would be a one-shot deal; there would be no long term contract with MGM. He knew he needed to secure something steady in movies after shooting *The Wizard of Oz*. Reluctantly, Fields turned down the offer and was replaced in the role by Frank Morgan.[12]

The situation with Buddy Ebsen was much more dire. Shortly after filming began, Ebsen inhaled some of the silver dust used for the Tin Man makeup and developed a serious lung issue that hospitalized him. He was replaced in the film by Jack Haley. Ebsen fully recovered, of course, and went on to a very long and successful career in movies and, especially, TV in the iconic roles of Jed Clampett and Barnaby Jones before his death in 2003 at the age of 95.

As far as Judy Garland's own feelings about the project, it was an opportunity to star in an MGM musical designed for her talents, but at the time she had no way of knowing it would eventually become one of the most important movies ever made. In fact, Garland was distracted by her current romance with bandleader Artie Shaw, attending events with him and sometimes accompanied by Shaw's good friend, comedian Phil Silvers, who would later become iconic himself as TV's Sergeant Bilko. Garland adored Silvers and thought he was the funniest man in the world.

It almost seems superfluous to outline the plot of so notable a movie as *The Wizard of Oz*. It involves young Dorothy Gale, who is bored and restless on her Uncle Henry and Auntie Em's farm, and its bleak, desolate surroundings. While her aunt and uncle are kind, and their farm hands are friendly, her only real companion is her dog, Toto,

The Films of Judy Garland

After several hits and misses, the principal cast included Jack Haley, Bert Lahr, Frank Morgan, Judy Garland, and Ray Bolger.

which is constantly being threatened by the bitter and angry Miss Gulch. A dreamer, Dorothy longs to leave her dull surroundings and travel over the rainbow to a place that is colorful and exciting. A cyclone strikes and Dorothy and Toto are whisked away, house and all, to a bright, colorful land called Oz that is run by a wizard, terrorized by a wicked witch, and filled with singing little people. Dorothy and Toto meet three friendly characters, a scarecrow who wants a brain, a tin man who desires a heart, and a cowardly lion who longs for courage. They, along with Dorothy, who just wants to find her way back home, follow a yellow brick road to find the Wizard with the belief that he can grant all of their wishes. Along the way they are confronted by the evil exploits of the Wicked Witch, who kidnaps Dorothy with the aid of an army of flying monkeys that are under her command. The Witch's anger is two-fold—she despises Dorothy because, upon landing in Oz, the house

The Early Years—*The Wizard of Oz* (1939)

transporting her landed on the Witch's sister, killing her. She also wants a pair of ruby slippers that had belonged to her sister and were placed on Dorothy by Glinda, a good witch who was the first to greet Dorothy as she entered Oz.

Those are the basics of the movie's plot. The elements that are contained therein, which form the narrative, are a series of scenes and episodes that employ action, excitement, humor, and a lot of music—many of the songs, composed by Harold Arlen and Yip Harburg, becoming as iconic in their own right as the movie. Thus, what this chapter will do is explore the film's elements, especially as they pertain to Judy Garland, and discuss just why it is such a remarkable film and so important to Garland's life and legacy.

It is not certain that the idea to film the Kansas sequences in sepia tone often presented in standard black and white and the Oz sequences in color was inspired by the 1933 Ted Eshbaugh cartoon. Eshbaugh directed a seven-minute *The Wizard of Oz* cartoon based on the Baum story with the opening Kansas sequences in black and white, switching to Technicolor upon Dorothy's arrival in Oz. It would stand to reason that this format inspired MGM to do the same, but it is not certain that producers Mervyn LeRoy or Arthur Freed ever saw the cartoon. It was never released. The Technicolor process it used was under exclusive contract with Walt Disney Studios, thus preventing the Eshbaugh film from being released at the time. It isn't impossible that the MGM producers attended a screening of the film, but there has been no confirmation that this ever occurred.

Originally, Richard Thorpe was set to direct *The Wizard of Oz*, and his vision was quite different than what transpired. The Wicked Witch was going to be sexy and alluring like the evil stepmother in Disney's *Snow White and the Seven Dwarfs*. Gale Sondergaard was hired to play the role. When the idea was changed to make the witch traditionally ugly, test shots with Sondergaard didn't work out. She left the project and was replaced by Margaret Hamilton two days before production started. Dorothy was also different; Garland was originally fitted with a blonde wig, makeup, and different clothing. Producer Mervyn LeRoy and his assistant Arthur Freed (who would later produce several important MGM musicals) were dissatisfied with Thorpe's approach and removed him from the project. George Cukor stepped in briefly, and while he didn't direct any footage (as he was assigned to start work on *Gone with the Wind*), he altered the makeup on the main characters and changed Dorothy's look to the one seen in the film. Though he only

Offscreen Margaret Hamilton was a sweet, kind lady, and Judy Garland had trouble reacting in fear to her portrayal of the Wicked Witch.

made a marginal and uncredited contribution, Cukor altered the entire visual concept of the major characters, reminding Garland that she was playing a much younger girl who was innocent and from Kansas. Garland had to wear an uncomfortable harness beneath her clothing

The Early Years—*The Wizard of Oz* (1939)

because she was nearing seventeen and playing a girl of around twelve, so her physical development had to be hidden.

Although the Kansas scenes open the film, they were filmed last, and not by Victor Fleming. By the time these scenes were shot, Fleming also had to leave the project and report to the set of *Gone with the Wind*. That film's star, Clark Gable, was not connecting well with George Cukor and insisted he be replaced with Fleming. As a result, director King Vidor helmed the Kansas sequences. Vidor had a knack for bleak visuals, and it was perhaps his film *Our Daily Bread*, which dealt with farm life, that inspired MGM to use him in place of Fleming. Vidor was good friends with Fleming, so he did the three weeks of work without taking credit. In fact, he didn't even admit to having done the work until after Victor Fleming had died.

The way the film is structured allows us to realize the likelihood of it all being a dream, so the conclusion isn't a surprise. However, the way it is presented is quite brilliant. In the Kansas scenes, Dorothy confronts her aunt and uncle, who are too busy to give her much attention, talks about intelligence with farmhand Hunk; sees another hand, Hickory, talk about emotion and having a statue dedicated to him; and is rescued by a third hand, Zeke, when she tumbles into a pigsty, and it is revealed that he is as frightened as she is. Their transformations into a scarecrow desiring a brain, a tin man wishing for a heart, and a cowardly lion longing for courage follows her train of logic. Of course, mean old Miss Gulch, who has a court order to take the dog Toto away, becomes the Wicked Witch, while a traveling entertainer full of phony tall tales becomes the ersatz wizard.

After being blown off casually by all of the adults in her world, and not having any friends her own age to confide in, Dorothy longs to leave the bleakness of Kansas and travel to a far-off place that lies over the rainbow, cuing the song. This musical number was nearly cut from the film, because it was believed that it stops the film's momentum and slows down the action. Fortunately, cooler heads prevailed and the song remained in the film. It not only achieved the same level of iconic status as the movie itself, it became a showstopping standard part of Garland's live act years later. And while the steady pace of the opening scenes might be sidetracked briefly by a tangential song number, it does have lyrics that reveal Dorothy's true feelings about her status in life.

While "Over the Rainbow" was very nearly cut from the movie, there are other scenes that were indeed jettisoned. One was "The Jitterbug" sequence, which was a jazzy number that connected with a current dance trend. Another was a lengthy dance number by Ray Bolger that really showed off his limber agility. When this sequence was discovered in the MGM vaults, it was considered so delightful that most fans wondered why it was edited out. The claim was that the film was too long. Even if both of these sequences were kept in the film, *The Wizard of Oz* still would not have been a very long movie, especially since it uses every second of its footage so well.

The munchkins were, for the most part, played by a group called the Singer Midgets, who got their name not because they sang, but because they were managed by a Mr. Singer. In fact, many little people who played munchkins could not sing, or even speak English, so their singing and speaking voices were dubbed. The group was dotted with noted little people actors like Jerry Maren, Meinhardt Raabe, Billy Curtis, and Harry Earles, and those with long careers on stage in vaudeville.

The colorful Oz is so filled with stimulating visuals, odd-but-kind friends, and cheerful songs that the evil witch who desires the ruby slippers doesn't seem all that threatening. She appears to be acting alone,

Traveling down the Yellow Brick Road.

The Early Years—*The Wizard of Oz* (1939)

until it is revealed that she has several flying monkeys as her minions. Still, with all of her bluster and intimidation, she is easily destroyed by a splash of water. Dorothy's imagination allows her to triumph with little effort. It is also easy to leave Oz and return to Kansas by merely clicking her heels together, but only after her exploits help her to realize her bleak, dreary farm world is the best place for her.

However, many children found the Witch and her flying monkeys to be very scary. They responded to them as a dark stain on this otherwise colorful and happy world. The Witch may be easily defeated in actuality, but all her bluster was found by some to be very intimidating, thanks in large part to Hamilton's performance.

Many, including director John Waters, have taken some umbrage at this film's denouement. Why would Dorothy want to leave a colorful place filled with music and excitement for her drab farm? And wouldn't that court order to take Toto away still hold once she awakens in the same situation? Of course, a fantasy film doesn't need this level of logical overthinking in order to enjoy and appreciate it.

While Judy Garland's daughters, Liza Minnelli and Lorna Luft, have recalled in interviews that their mother fondly remembered working on the film as a pleasurable experience, Jack Haley in later years would indicate how proud he was to be a part of such a classic, but also state, "When people come up to me and say it must have been fun to make that picture, I tell them no, it was not fun, it was a lot of really hard work!"[13] Jack Haley, unable to bend or sit in his cumbersome Tin Man costume, had a special rack that he could lean against and rest during scenes, where he'd hang and take a nap. This always impressed insomniac Bert Lahr.

The Wizard of Oz enjoyed widespread praise from the critics. In the trade magazine *Movies and the People Who Make Them*, their critic stated:

> Comparable only to *Snow White and the Seven Dwarfs* and yet completely different in tone and treatment and being not a cartoon but a flesh-and-blood fairy tale, *The Wizard of Oz* is probably the most expensive film and certainly one of the most entertaining films of 1939. It is a shrewd mixture of childish fantasy, adult satire, and ageless homespun humor. Its screenplay preserves the flavor of the originals and combines the best features of both the book, which has sold during forty years more than 10,000,000 copies, and the musical comedy in which Fred Stone, Anna Laughlin, and Dave Montgomery toured for four years after 18 months on Broadway. Its presentation displays both imagination and painstaking care. And its production is lavish and

resplendent in every respect. Judy Garland is a natural and appealing Dorothy with eyes that can see wonderment with belief. *The Wizard of Oz* is an American fairy tale made into a memorable American movie.[14]

Surprisingly, however, *The Wizard of Oz* was not a box office success upon its initial release. To ensure widespread notice and appeal, MGM held its premiere in Green Bay, Wisconsin, and sneak previewed it in that state's cities like Kenosha and Oconomowoc before holding its Hollywood premiere at Grauman's Chinese Theater with Garland and Mickey Rooney performing live ahead of time. In fact, Garland and Rooney toured with the film for a week, providing a live action opening that also promoted the film they were working on together, *Babes in Arms*. Garland performed live for a second week, accompanied by Ray Bolger and Bert Lahr. It was during these test screenings that the two-hour movie seemed to be too long, thus resulting in the removal of

Before he left to begin work on *Gone with the Wind*, director Victor Fleming had a birthday celebration on the set of *The Wizard of Oz* with Judy Garland, Myrna Loy (who was visiting the set), and Frank Morgan.

The Early Years—*The Wizard of Oz* (1939)

"The Jitterbug" sequence, Ray Bolger's extended dance, and some other moments in order to tighten the film. It is also when "Over the Rainbow" was nearly removed.

The budget for *The Wizard of Oz* was $2.8 million, and in its first theatrical run it only made around $3 million. When including the roughly $300,000 of promotion and distribution costs, *The Wizard of Oz* actually lost money and was considered a box office disappointment. Part of the reason could be that the movie was so expensive to make and so many of the people who went to see it were children who got in for cheaper admission that it wasn't enough to turn a profit. It didn't start making money until it was reissued in 1949, and then again in 1955. While the 1949 reissue retained the sepia tone for the Kansas scenes, beginning in 1955 this sequence was presented in standard black and white. The sepia tone was restored many years later.

The Wizard of Oz really achieved iconic status after MGM sold the television rights to CBS for $225,000 per broadcast, which happened for the first time on November 3, 1956. It was a huge ratings success. The film was shown again in December of 1959, garnering an even greater viewing audience. It was then that it became an annual television tradition. For many generations, viewers would look forward to its annual broadcast. Taking into consideration how much of the film was lost on the TV screens of that era, which were, on average, around 19 inches and only telecast in black and white, it really shows that the heart of the film and its fine performances transcend such limitations.

The film was eventually released to home video on VHS and Betamax in October of 1980, on Laser Disc in 1983, and on DVD in 1997. Its first Blu-ray release was in 2009. The film has been released in several different packages over the years, commemorating different anniversaries. Sometimes extras in the video packages contain the early silent Oz adaptions, including a restored version of the Larry Semon 1925 feature and the Ted Eshbaugh cartoon. The film was also released to theaters over the years, including a one-night-only showing in 2009 with the sepia footage returned after over 50 years.

While it could be argued that Garland was a little too old for this role, she really embodied the kindness and innocence required for a character like Dorothy, combined with a bit of spunk. She never hesitates to stand up for her friends or for what she believes is the right thing to do. Her performance and the film's message of belonging are timeless and a big reason why this film is so widely seen over 80 years after its release. It's so steeped in popular culture that many people can probably recognize a song like "Over the Rainbow" or a quote like "There's no place like home" immediately, even if they have never seen the movie. And even though color has been the norm for movies for many decades, that sense of wonder when Dorothy opens the door and the movie transitions from sepia to color is forever awe-inspiring.

Despite its initial box office disappointment, *The Wizard of Oz* had a major impact on Judy Garland's career. At the next Academy Awards ceremony, she was given an Honorary Oscar for performances in this film and in her next, *Babes in Arms*. Her hard work showed MGM that she was a formidable enough presence to stand out in an ensemble, as well as co-star with a powerhouse like Mickey Rooney, with whom she had strong on-screen chemistry. In fact, she was still doing retakes on *The Wizard of Oz* when she was cast opposite Rooney in *Babes in Arms*, which became her next film.

Babes in Arms

Directed by Busby Berkeley
Screenplay by Jack McGowan and Kay Van Riper (based on the play by Richard Rodgers and Lorenz Hart)
Produced by Arthur Freed
Cinematography by Ray June
Film editing by Frank Sullivan
Songs:
  "Babes in Arms"; Music by Richard Rodgers; Lyrics by Lorenz Hart
  "Where or When"; Music by Richard Rodgers; Lyrics by Lorenz Hart
  "Good Morning"; Music by Nacio Herb Brown; Lyrics by Arthur Freed
  "God's Country"; Music by Harold Arlen; Lyrics by E.Y. Harburg
  "You Are My Lucky Star"; Music by Nacio Herb Brown; Lyrics by Arthur Freed
  "I Like Opera/I Like Swing"; Composer unknown
  "Figaro"; Words and music by Roger Edens
  "Broadway Rhythm"; Music by Nacio Herb Brown; Lyrics by Arthur Freed

The Early Years—*Babes in Arms* (1939)

"I Cried for You"; Written by Gus Arnheim, Abe Lyman, and Arthur Freed
"My Daddy Was a Minstrel Man"; Written by Roger Edens
"Oh! Susanna"; Written by Stephen Foster
"Mr. Bones and Mr. Tambo"; Words and Music by Roger Edens
"Ida! Sweet as Apple Cider"; Music by Eddie Munson; Lyrics by Eddie Leonard
"Moonlight Bay"; Music by Percy Wenrich; Lyrics by Edward Madden
"I'm Just Wild About Harry"; Music by Eubie Blake; Lyrics by Noble Sissle
"Bob White Whatcha Gonna Swing Tonight?"; Music by Bernard Hanighen; Lyrics by Johnny Mercer
Cast: Mickey Rooney, Judy Garland, Charles Winniger, Guy Kibbee, June Preisser, Grace Hayes, Betty Jaynes, Douglas McPhail, Rand Brooks, Leni Lynn, Johnny Sheffield, Henry Hull, Barnet Parker, Ann Shoemaker, Margaret Hamilton, Joseph Crehan, George McKay, Henry Roquemore, Lelah Taylor, Charles D. Brown, George F. Calger, Jr., Frank Darien, James Donalan, Sidney Miller, Libby Taylor, Joe Caits, Dick Dennis, Robert Emmett Keane, Lon McCallister, Cyril Ring, Charles Smith, Mary Treen, Pat West, Frank Whitbeck, Robert Winkler, Leonard Sues, Inna Gest, Ann Bupp, and Lois James
Released October 13, 1939
Metro Goldwyn Mayer
94 minutes
Black and White

Babes in Arms became something of a legendary film in that it is the first one where the adolescent offspring of showbiz parents decided to put on their own show in a barn. Arthur Freed, who had worked on *The Wizard of Oz* in support of producer Mervyn LeRoy, was given full producing control over this film, and its success ignited his career. Mickey Rooney, with his unbridled enthusiasm, received an Oscar nomination. And *Babes in Arms* became one of the most popular films of 1939.

Babes in Arms had been a Broadway show, running 289 performances first at the Shubert Theater, and then the Majestic. It starred Dan Dailey, Mitzi Green, and the Nicholas Brothers. Arthur Freed, then head of MGM's music department, suggested to Louis B. Mayer that a screen version of *Babes in Arms* might be a good musical for Mickey

The Films of Judy Garland

Rooney and Judy Garland. Freed had done well with his production duties on *The Wizard of Oz*, and Mervyn LeRoy let Mayer know how much his insights were helpful to that project. As soon as his work on *The Wizard of Oz* ended, while King Vidor was shooting the Kansas sequences, Freed began putting together this project. Of course, Judy Garland was still working on *The Wizard of Oz*, but began recording songs for *Babes in Arms*. Mickey Rooney recalled:

> I remember when we were recording the songs for the picture. Judy had to get in costume to do retakes on *Wizard of Oz*, and then hurried to the sound department to record a duet with me for *Babes in Arms*. So here I am singing a song with Judy in her Dorothy costume, including the pigtails.[15]

Babes in Arms has Mickey Moran (Mickey Rooney) and his friend Patsy (Judy Garland) as the children of vaudeville performers whose time in the spotlight has been fading. The actors aren't well liked or appreciated in their community due to the prejudice against show folk permeating the area. There is concern that the children aren't getting a decent education because they have to keep leaving school to travel with their parents on tours. Community leaders want the children placed in boarding schools but, fortunately, the judge respects the work ethic of show people and dismisses these concerns. At just the right time, a booking agent decides to put together a revival variety show featuring veteran vaudeville performers, to celebrate both the nostalgia and the history of the art form. Mickey and Patsy, along with the offspring of the other performers in the show, are excited about a new tour. Mickey is especially enthusiastic because a song he wrote was recently accepted by a music publisher, netting him $100. However, the youngsters are heartbroken upon being told that they will not be a part of the tour, and will be staying behind. Boldly, they decide to put together their own show.

The narrative is basically about vaudeville veterans trying to maintain in an ever-changing showbiz while their children represent the future by putting together their own, more immediately relevant show. Mickey Rooney and Judy Garland are the stars of the film, so their sub-plot becomes the narrative's center. It shows Mickey with the very grown-up problem of having to put a semi-skilled young lady named Rosalie (June Preisser) in the lead because she is wealthy and has agreed to finance the show. Rosalie used to be a child star and is looking for the opportunity to reclaim that status, just as the vaudeville parents are trying to keep their style relevant. This relegates Patsy to understudy,

The Early Years—*Babes in Arms* (1939)

Mickey Rooney and Judy Garland put on a show in *Babes in Arms*.

and also underscores the Rooney-Garland relationship in all of their films, where a supportive, understanding, and sacrificing Garland never gets the level of appreciation or affection from the driven Rooney. Patsy is not unlike Betsy Booth in the Andy Hardy movies. Patsy does what is best for the show and remains loyal to Mickey, but her heartbreak is evident to the audience.

Patsy is a bit different from the Betsy Booth character in that she is seen as a little more mature; to Mickey, she is an equal. He kisses her at the very beginning of the movie, and they work together on equal terms. She is not someone he sees as a little girl, even if he is momentarily distracted from her by someone like Rosalie. Therefore, it feels like a much more appropriate role for Garland at this point in her career.

This part of the narrative is given heightened conflict when Patsy walks in on Mickey kissing Rosalie, not realizing it is just part of a scene they're rehearsing. Patsy scurries away in tears and takes the next train to meet her parents at their next vaudeville engagement. When she weeps her problem to her mother, Patsy is told that in show business, one doesn't allow emotions to disrupt one's work in a show, so Patsy returns. On the night of the show, Rosalie's father yanks his daughter out of the production, believing a local review is beneath her. This allows understudy Patsy to go on.

While it is nearly impossible to co-star with Mickey Rooney and not have him overshadow all that are nearby, Judy Garland always holds her own at his level, and that is why MGM liked teaming them. They were offscreen pals, so no jealousies arose during their performances.

Babes in Arms really does spotlight the Patsy character as much as Mickey. Judy Garland had explored a lot of different opportunities in her myriad of movie roles thus far, so a layered character like Patsy was something she could perform quite effectively. The role gives her an opportunity to sing, dance, and play a character that connects deeply with the viewer—we feel her longing, her disappointment, and her triumph because Garland performs those emotions so well. Patsy is every bit as strong and complex a character as Dorothy Gale had been, and Garland's performance is just as magical and impressive.

Of course, the wrap-up concentrates somewhat more on Mickey, and, in typical MGM fashion, the story hits a low before rising above it and ending the film on a high. Mickey's show is being performed outdoors. A hurricane moves in and forces it to end early. The parents return home early because their tour had ended due to poor attendance. Then suddenly, Mickey hears from a theatrical producer who saw his show and wants to start a tour. The parents are hired to help on the project and all is well.

It is notable that Charles Winninger has an especially poignant moment as Mickey's father Joe. Joe is one of those vaudeville performers who is struggling to find work as the entertainment industry changes, to the point where toward the end of the movie he disappears, supposedly out looking for a more stable job and giving up performing for the first time in his life. When the producer offers him a job on Mickey's show so he doesn't have to leave show business, he appears greatly moved, and it's really heartbreaking and briefly steals the movie from Rooney and Garland.

There are a few dated, unsettling elements in the film's finale. A minstrel performance that the gang puts on before the hurricane takes up a large part of the movie, and as discussed in the chapter for *Everybody Sing*, while blackface wasn't at all unusual in the 1930s, it can be rather disturbing in the 21st century. Even the patriotism of the "God's Country" finale is negated by some stereotyping. But it does show how

The Early Years—*Babes in Arms* (1939)

well director Busby Berkeley was able to adapt to this new type of musical that was quite different from the backstage stories with big kaleidoscopic numbers, as found in his earlier films like *42nd Street* (1932) and *Footlight Parade* (1933).

Busby Berkeley was working in a much different atmosphere than he was used to. According to Hugh Fordin's book *The World of Entertainment*:

> It was a different world for Berkeley than his days at Warner Brothers. No longer was a musical to be built around a backstage plot where the musical number is staged as a formal spectacle. In Arthur Freed's hands, the musical number became part and parcel of the story. The picture's budget was another factor and Berkeley, therefore, had to deal with a more intimate space since he didn't have at his disposal a huge area in which to display sixty or eighty girls. Moreover, he was now faced with the interplay of characters, woven into the texture of the musical picture.[16]

Babes in Arms was a difficult shoot for Judy Garland. She didn't get along well with Busby Berkeley, and was struggling due to having no time to rest between the hard work on *The Wizard of Oz* and the equally hard work on *Babes in Arms*. The fact that she and Rooney were assigned to perform live at showings of *The Wizard of Oz* right after completing *Babes in Arms* made things even more daunting. At one point, Garland collapsed backstage and had to be revived while Rooney did a solo for a few minutes. On November 9, 1941, radio's *Screen Guild Theater* broadcast a 30-minute adaptation of the movie with Mickey Rooney and Judy Garland reprising their film roles. Biographies claim that this is around the time that Garland was given pills to keep her energy, which led to her needing pills to unwind so she could sleep.

Babes in Arms wasn't a completely faithful adaption of the Broadway show. MGM preferred to put their own songs in the musicals they produced, so only three of the Rodgers and Hart compositions from the original Broadway show ended up in the movie—the title tune, "Where or When," and "The Lady Is a Tramp," the latter only heard in the background. Others were composed specifically for this film.

MGM knew it had a hit with *Babes in Arms* when it received major accolades from a tough audience at the film's Hollywood premiere. Mickey Rooney recalled:

> We didn't realize then it would become such a big hit, or that it would be the first in a series of backyard musicals. After the premiere ended, Judy cried when she heard the applause. We were just two kids who worked hard and now we are being applauded by all of Hollywood.[17]

The Films of Judy Garland

The budget for *Babes in Arms* was less than $750,000 and grossed over $3 million. It was the year's biggest moneymaker for its cost.

The critics also took notice in all the trades as well as the major newspapers, thus further ensuring box office success. *Variety* stated:

> Despite the Rooney dominance throughout, there are several sterling performances by the younger talent. Judy Garland most effectively carries the adolescent romantic interest opposite him.[18]

The response of moviegoers was presented by exhibitors' comments in the trade magazine *Box Office*, For *Babes in Arms*, the comments included:

> Pleased 100% and drew considerable extra business. This was Mickey's greatest opportunity and he didn't miss a step. Judy is mighty fine by herself too.
> Enjoyed by all. Some saw it twice.
> This swell piece of entertainment really brought in the shekels for us.
> Rooney proved himself a real trouper. The Garland kid was right behind him all the way. She has more rooters with each picture.[19]

Judy Garland's success was strong and impactful, but the grueling schedule resulted in her first collapse from overwork and reportedly her first experience with pills to help her through. At least she got a bit of a rest before going into her next two productions, both with Mickey Rooney. MGM wanted another musical to star the duo, so Gershwin's *Strike Up the Band* was being prepared. It also wanted Garland in the next Andy Hardy movie, so she shot a few scenes as Betsy Booth around February and March 1940 for *Andy Hardy Meets Debutante* while already starting work on *Strike Up the Band*.

At the same time, Garland's personal life started to become more complicated. Her mother wouldn't allow her to see Artie Shaw, so she had her pal and former boyfriend Jackie Cooper act as though he was dating her again, so she could sneak off with Shaw. However, just as she was about to start work on her next movie projects and embark on another grueling schedule, Garland read headlines stating that Shaw had eloped with Lana Turner. It broke her heart. She sobbed to her mother and called Phil Silvers, a friend of both Shaw and Garland, and cried to him as well. It was a shock because she understood that Shaw and Turner didn't even like each other.

Judy Garland had experienced in real life what her Betsy Booth-type characters endured on the screen. Pleasantly attractive Garland was no match for the sex appeal of someone like Lana Turner.

The Early Years—*Andy Hardy Meets Debutante* (1940)

Andy Hardy Meets Debutante

Directed by George B. Seitz
Screenplay by Aurania Rouverol, Thomas Seller, and Annalee Whitmore
Produced by J.J. Cohn
Cinematography by Charles Lawton, Jr., and Sidney Wagner
Film editing by Harold F. Kress
Songs:
 "Alone"; Music by Nacio Herb Brown; Lyrics by Arthur Freed
 "I'm Nobody's Baby"; Written by Benny Davis, Milton Ager, and Lester Santley
Cast: Mickey Rooney, Judy Garland, Lewis Stone, Fay Holden, Cecilia Parker, Ann Rutherford, Diana Lewis, Addison Richards, Clyde Wilson, Cy Kendall, George Lessey, Claire Du Brey, Marjorie Gateson, John Merkyl, Charles Trowbridge, Herbert Evans, and Edwin Stanley
Released July 5, 1940
Metro Goldwyn Mayer
88 minutes
Black and White

Although he would continue for many more films, Mickey Rooney was beginning to tire of the Hardy series by the time he made *Andy Hardy Meets Debutante*. But in a 2001 interview with the author, Rooney understood why he and Garland were quickly shunted into another Hardy movie.

> I had done *Boys Town*. Judy had done *The Wizard of Oz*. We both did *Babes in Arms*. All big pictures. I was nominated for an Oscar. Judy and I both received special Oscars. So, when we went into another Hardy picture, it was small budgets, the same type stories, and just another way for the studio to make a pile of money. But we did our jobs.[20]

And while Garland was once again clearly in support, and was yet again the tangential friend, not the girl friend, it is her Betsy Booth character that not only saves the day, but has a better understanding of the situation in a small town in which Andy Hardy finds himself.

In this one, Andy Hardy becomes smitten with New York debutante Daphne Fowler, whose image he has seen in magazines. He clips out her pictures and places them in a scrapbook, looking through it longingly at every opportunity. Although he has never met Daphne Fowler, Andy loftily believes he is more sophisticated than his small town friends, including girlfriend Polly Benedict. He plans to break up with her, but she breaks up with him first, believing he is too juvenile. Offended, Andy tries to flaunt his sophistication by claiming to be dating Daphne Fowler. When Judge Hardy is called to New York on business, Polly and Beezy, her co-editor on the school paper, insist Andy prove his claim by returning with a picture of Daphne Fowler and him together. Andy worries about being found out until he arrives in New York and visits Betsy Booth, who lives there. It turns out that Betsy, who travels with a wealthier crowd, is actually good friends with Daphne and makes arrangements for the photograph that Polly and Beezy dared Andy to get.

The dynamic between Betsy and Andy has her in control. While he perceives himself as a sophisticate, Andy is merely a big fish in a small

Judy Garland as Betsy Booth comes to the rescue of Mickey Rooney as Andy Hardy in *Andy Hardy Meets Debutante.*

The Early Years—*Andy Hardy Meets Debutante* (1940)

pond—his homespun, small-town naïveté needing support and wisdom from the big city-bred, worldly Betsy. For instance, when Andy goes to have lunch at a swanky restaurant that Daphne Fowler is known to frequent, Betsy tries to explain that it is quite expensive. Andy is not worried, naïvely stating, "I have eight dollars on me." Andy continually dismisses Betsy as a child who couldn't possibly understand his grown-up situation, but it is she who saves the day. When Andy does reveal the details of his plight, and it is revealed that this mystery socialite is her old pal Daphne, she goes directly to a nearby phone and calls her. Bumpkin Andy is summed up pretty well when, at one point, Judge Hardy states, "When a boy is stupid, he's just stupid, and there isn't much one can do."

Perhaps the major highlight in *Andy Hardy Meets Debutante* is when a dejected Betsy Booth sings, "I'm Nobody's Baby," which soon became a hit song for Judy Garland. The song lyrics even reference Clark Gable at one point, reminding one of her "Dear Mr. Gable" career triumph.

It is likely that Garland felt that going back to playing Betsy after starring in films like *The Wizard of Oz* and *Babes in Arms* felt like a step back for her, but she's really great in the music numbers in particular; "I'm Nobody's Baby" and "Alone" feel like more mature numbers in which she's literally claiming that she's not a baby. And Andy is enthralled watching her perform.

Andy Hardy Meets Debutante was made for just over $400,000 and grossed nearly $3 million. MGM had no plans to discontinue the series despite Mickey Rooney's losing interest in playing the character. And although she just had a small, supporting part, Judy Garland now had the career impact to help a film's box office. *Variety* stated:

> With second appearance of Judy Garland in the series indicating that she might move in for regular assignment later, if the Rooney-Garland duo might be required to strengthen later issues. Miss Garland is prominent and lovely as the adoring girlfriend in the big city.[21]

Garland was still recovering from the shock of Artie Shaw marrying Lana Turner. According to her biographer, Garland's mother called Shaw, irate at how he hurt her daughter. Shaw was taken aback and explained that Garland was only a friend, and there was never any sexual relationship. Garland apparently thought there was more to the relationship. Just like her Betsy Booth character in the Hardy movies, Shaw considered Garland a cute friend, while someone like Lana Turner was the type a guy married. Lana would be one of eight marriages for Shaw, and their marriage would last only a few months.

After shooting her scenes for *Andy Hardy Meets Debutante*, Garland had more time to devote to *Strike Up the Band*, which was a much more important film. MGM wanted to recapture the box office success of *Babes in Arms,* and realized the combination of Mickey Rooney and Judy Garland had a great deal of box office power. But they also knew that both Rooney and Garland had proven they could carry a movie on their own. Future plans for Garland would be to spotlight her in her own vehicles.

Strike Up the Band

Directed by Busby Berkeley
Screenplay by Fred F. Finklehoffe and John Monks, Jr.
Produced by Arthur Freed
Cinematography by Ray June
Film editing by Ben Lewis
Songs:
"Strike up the Band"; Music by George Gershwin; Lyrics by Ira Gershwin
"Our Love Affair"; Music by Roger Edens; Lyrics by Arthur Freed
"Do the La Conga"; Music and lyrics by Roger Edens
"Nobody"; Music and lyrics by Roger Edens
"The Gay Nineties"; Music and lyrics by Roger Edens
"Nell of New Rochelle"; Music and lyrics by Roger Edens
"A Man Was the Cause of It All"; Music and lyrics by Roger Edens
"Heaven Will Protect the Working Girl"; Music by A. Baldwin Sloane; Lyrics by Edgar Smith
"Ta-ra-ra Boom-der-é"; Written by Henry J. Sayers
"Come Home, Father (1864)"; Music and lyrics by Henry Clay Work
"When Day is Done (1926)"; Music by Robert Katscher
"Wonderful One (1922)"; Music by Paul Whiteman and Ferde Grofé, Sr.
"Drummer Boy (1939)"; Music by Roger Edens; Lyrics by Roger Edens and Arthur Freed

The Early Years—*Strike Up the Band* (1940)

Cast: Mickey Rooney, Judy Garland, Paul Whiteman, June Preisser, William Tracy, Larry Nunn, Margaret Early, Ann Shoemaker, Francis Pierlot, Virginia Brissac, Harry McCrillis, George Lessey, Enid Bennett, Howard Hickman, Sarah Edwards, Joe Yule, Virginia Sale, Henry Roquemore, Dick Paxton, Sherrie Overton, Margaret Marquis, Vondell Darr, Jack Albertson, Sidney Miller, and Jack Mulhall

Note: Phil Silvers appeared as a pitchman during the carnival scene, but his footage was deleted before release.

Released September 27, 1940
Metro-Goldwyn-Mayer
120 Minutes
Black and White

In 1940, Judy Garland had reached a lofty level of stardom. She received an honorary miniature Oscar, was given a $10,000 bonus for her hard work and success during 1939, and was signed to a new contract. According to a syndicated article in the press:

> Judy Garland moved into the ranks of Hollywood's best paid actresses with a contract which will pay near $2,000 a week for the first three years of a seven-year option. The 18-year-old singing star went to court Thursday for approval of her new contract. Judge William S. Baird awarded her $500 a week for living expenses. Under the agreement with Metro-Goldwyn-Mayer, Miss Garland also will receive half the revenue from radio programs on which she appears.[22]

And the studio had plans to star her in her own vehicles, where she did not share the lead with another actor or ensemble. But first she had to finish work on *Strike Up the Band*.

Garland's professional life was going well, but her personal life had at least one unsettling incident that showed the perils of stardom. A 19-year-old plotted to kidnap the 17-year-old actress. An article in the *Los Angeles Times* stated:

> Sixteen police officers last night were guarding the home of Judy Garland, juvenile screen and stage star, after a mysterious informant telephoned a Culver City police sergeant and said the youthful actress would be kidnaped. Two of the squad of officers were assigned as personal bodyguards for the 17-year-old MGM studio starlet. The singing actress was at home with her sister Virginia and six other youthful friends when police arrived but was unable to give any clue as to the reason for the threat. She told detectives she had never received any threats. Miss Garland's mother, Mrs. Ethel Gumm Gilmore, who was married last Nov. 18 in Yuma to William P. Gilmore, was reported to be visiting friends in Santa Cruz with her husband.[23]

The Films of Judy Garland

Garland was calm and continued to entertain her company, even to the point of having ice cream brought to the police who were guarding her. The suspect later claimed he didn't really want to kidnap Garland; he just wanted to meet her. He was held for mental evaluation.

MGM was planning on co-starring Mickey Rooney and Judy Garland in the musical *Good News*, but Louis B. Mayer liked the patriotic theme of *Strike Up the Band*, from the George and Ira Gershwin Broadway musical, and ordered that a film version be made. The subsequent film has nothing to do with the Gershwin show, a political satire, and only retained the title and the title song from the Broadway production. *Good News* would eventually be made by MGM in 1947 with June Allyson and Peter Lawford co-starring in the roles that were intended for Garland and Rooney.

Strike Up the Band features Mickey Rooney as Jimmy Connors, a typically enthusiastic teenage dreamer whose mother wants him to be a doctor like his late father, but who longs to become a bandleader with his own orchestra. Judy Garland is Mary Holden, yet another character

June Preisser distracts Mickey Rooney from Judy Garland in *Strike Up the Band*.

The Early Years—*Strike Up the Band* (1940)

in the typical Garland-Rooney dynamic. Mary longs for Jimmy, while his focus is on his ambitious plans, and he never sees Mary as more than a pal. Jimmy manages to convince his school principal to allow him to take over the student orchestra and make it a swing band. After enjoying success in their small town community, Jimmy decides he wants to raise $200 to get his band to Chicago to audition for bandleader Paul Whiteman playing himself. Suddenly a new girl moves into the community, giggly Barbara, who disrupts the connection between Jimmy and Mary—a role similar to Rosalie in *Babes in Arms* and played by the same actress, June Preisser. The chief dramatic tension in the narrative happens when one of the gang, Willie,[24] who has a puppy love crush on Mary, breaks his arm badly. Jimmy gives up the $200 he earned for the Chicago trip in order to pay for a doctor for Willie. Since $50 of this money had been borrowed against Jimmy's drums as collateral, he makes the ultimate sacrifice for his friend. The film concludes with Barbara's wealthy father, a railroad magnate, arranging for a special train to get to Chicago in time for Jimmy's band to compete in Paul Whiteman's contest for high school bands. The band win the first prize of $500.

Strike Up the Band continued to display how well Mickey Rooney and Judy Garland worked together, but it is still more Mickey's movie than Judy's. While she is typically pleasant in her role as the overlooked wall flower, Garland really stands out during her musical numbers. Unlike *Babes in Arms*, where Rooney, Garland, and company were showbiz kids whose parents were also entertainers, in *Strike Up the Band* they were more typical high schoolers from non-showbiz families who didn't quite understand the kids' dreams. These are not ordinary working-class families—these are privileged rich kids who will be allowed every advantage, so the parents don't understand that the kids' goals are so dreamy and atypical. While Jimmy lives in a modest home with a single parent, Mary comes from real wealth and privilege. Still, they both have the same dream, and when Willie needs an operation, they fend for themselves regarding the money despite the level of sacrifice.

One particular scene in *Strike Up the Band* stands out as quite clever and interesting on a few different levels:

> As the dynamic between Jimmy and Mary is introduced and initially develops, there is a truly imaginative scene in which Jimmy, at Mary's house, takes a bowl of fruit and starts placing it around the table, showing the formation of the orchestra as it appears in his imagination. The scene then evolves into one where the fruit comes to life and starts playing instruments; a clever bit of

The Films of Judy Garland

Larry Nunn is smitten with Judy Garland, distracting her from Mickey Rooney in *Strike Up the Band*.

animation that is unusual for a movie such as this. This was the idea of a visitor to the set. Vincente Minnelli had just been hired by MGM as a director, and was visiting the set of *Strike Up the Band* producer Arthur Freed during filming. Freed casually mentioned to Minnelli that they needed a big production number at this point in the movie and couldn't come up with anything. Minnelli suggested the idea using fruit; the producer liked it, and asked animator George Pal to come up with something. It is one of the most unusual and amusing sequences in the film. Minnelli and Judy Garland would be married in another five years, their union resulting in their famous daughter Liza Minnelli.[25]

Another musical number that stood out, "La Conga Nights," was blown up considerably by Busby Berkeley's vision as director. Roger Edens recalled for Hugh Fordin:

> It started out simply as a song I had written for Judy to sing, based on the current dance craze, the conga. Then Berkeley got crazy and decided on blowing the whole number up into one of his typical finales, using every possible camera angle he could think up. Judy was done up like someone out of a Persian

The Early Years—*Strike Up the Band* (1940)

carnival for what was to be the last scene needed to complete the film. Berkeley then decided to complicate matters even further by announcing he would shoot the whole number in one take! With The Six Hits and a Miss, as a vocal backup for Judy, Paul Whiteman and his orchestra with Mickey on drums, and 115 dancers, Berkeley rehearsed his cast and crew for thirteen days and it was read. It worked. And without a hitch.[26]

This increased the budget to nearly $840,000, but the movie grossed over $3 million.

A dazzling, musical, seriocomic tale where the actors reach near bottom before making a successful comeback, the structure of *Strike Up the Band* is typical of MGM's approach. This was a real success at the box office, netting over a million dollars profit for the studio. Critics were impressed, with the *New York Times* stating:

> Roll out the red carpet, folks, and stand by. That boy is here again, the Pied Piper of the box offices, the eighth or ninth wonder of the world, the kid himself—in short, Mickey Rooney. With a capable assist by Judy Garland, Mr. Rooney strutted into the Capitol on Saturday at the head of "Strike Up the Band," and it should surprise no one this morning to learn that the show is his from beginning to end. For a boy of his years he has accumulated quite a bag of tricks and he will show them off at the tap of a drummer's stick. He charges about like the short-handed cast of an old stock melodrama. Mr. Rooney is having himself a time in this one, and—being the frantic actor that he is—chances are that everyone else will too.[27]

While *Variety* stated:

> *Strike Up the Band* is Metro's successor to "Babes in Arms," with Mickey Rooney, assisted by major trouping on the part of Judy Garland. Picture is overall smacko entertainment and Mickey Rooney teamed with Judy Garland is a wealth of effective entertainment.[28]

Judy Garland turned 18 during the filming of *Strike Up the Band* and on that date, she was given an engagement ring from her boyfriend, musician David Rose, whom she began seeing just after the Artie Shaw heartbreak. However, Rose was, at the time, still married to comedienne Martha Raye, although they were separated and had filed for divorce. They waited a year for Rose's divorce to become final, and married on July 27, 1941.

Meanwhile, Judy Garland was once again hard at work with no break. She was still finishing up work on *Andy Hardy Meets Debutante* when she began rehearsing for *Strike Up the Band*. And she was already starting rehearsals for her next movie, *Little Nellie Kelly*, before finishing her work on *Strike Up the Band*.

Little Nellie Kelly

Directed by Norman Taurog
Screenplay by Jack McGowan (based on the musical comedy by
   George M. Cohan)
Produced by Arthur Freed
Cinematography by Ray June
Film editing by Fredrick Y. Smith
Songs:
   "A Pretty Girl Milking Her Cow"; Music Adapted by Roger Edens;
      Lyrics by Roger Edens
   "It's a Great Day for the Irish"; Music and lyrics by Roger Edens
   "Singin' in the Rain"; Music by Nacio Herb Brown; Lyrics by
      Arthur Freed
   "Nellie Kelly I Love You"; Music and lyrics by George M. Cohan
Cast: Judy Garland, George Murphy, Charles Winninger, Douglas McPhail, Arthur Shields, Rita Page, Forrester Harvey, James Burke, George Watts, Barbara Bedford, Margaret Bert, Henry Blair, Tom Dillon, Robert Emmett Keane, Lee Phelps, George McKay, Howard Mitchell, Almira Sessions, Douglas Spencer, Cap Somers, Leslie Sketchley, Harry Semels, Paul Russell, Mel Ruick, Cyril Ring, Addison Richards, Bob Reeves, John Raitt, John Power, Pat O'Malley, Frank O'Connor, Anton Northpole, Norman Nielson, Edmund Mortimer, Pat Moriarty, Sidney Miller, Charles McAvoy, Cathy Lewis, Milton Kibbee, Dick Johnstone, Shep Houghton, Bob Ingersole, Perk Lazelle, Sven Hugo Borg, George Hoagland, Robert Bradford, Hubert Head, Robert Bradford, George Guhle, Helen Dickson, James Carlisle, Larry Clifford Joseph Crehan, Edward Biby, Ernie Alexander, and Bill Armstrong
Released November 22, 1940
Metro-Goldwyn-Mayer
98 Minutes
Black and White

Little Nellie Kelly is a pleasant trifle, by no means great cinema, and not as good a film as *Strike Up the Band*, much less *The Wizard of Oz*. However, *Little Nellie Kelly* was a very important film during this portion of Judy Garland's screen career. It was her first starring role, her

The Early Years—*Little Nellie Kelly* (1940)

first adult role, and it was a part that offered challenges beyond what she was called upon to do in previous movies. This was the studio's test as to whether Garland could carry a film in the title role as its star. She rose to the occasion, and *Little Nellie Kelly* was a box office smash, earning more than double its production costs. It was also an important hit for producer Arthur Freed, who would go on to make some of MGM's most memorable musicals.

The story is based on a 1920s play by George M. Cohan, who sold the rights to the studio, through Freed, with the understanding that it would be a vehicle for Judy Garland. Cohan himself realized the story would be quite dated for a 1940 movie, but Freed only wanted the gist of the story and the title song. For that, he still secured the movie rights from Cohan, a respected playwright.

Louis B. Mayer realized Cohan was a very patriotic Irish American, and the story of an Irish family who eagerly goes to America to find success and manages to do so was a premise that would be good for the studio as well as Mayer's own patriotism. However, Mayer balked at Garland playing an adult role. Frank Miller at the TCM website states:

> When Mayer heard of Freed's plans to star Judy Garland in the *Little Nellie Kelly* he protested, We simply can't have that baby have a child. Of course, that child was already 18, was firmly entrenched in the prescription-drug regimen that would ultimately destroy her career, was smoking four packs a day to keep her weight down and was running around in secret with a series of older men.[29]

Garland herself was eager to branch out into more grownup roles and star in the film.

Judy Garland plays the title character, Nellie, wife of Jerry Kelly (George Murphy), who longs to leave his native Ireland and settle in America where there is ample opportunity. He hopes to secure a job as a police officer in Manhattan. They are followed by Nellie's lazy-but-doting grandfather Michael Noonan (Charles Winninger), who grumpily opposes her marriage and her moving to America, mostly because he doesn't want to go to work. Jerry gets a job as a security guard and finally makes his way to policeman, as is his dream. Nellie gives birth to a daughter, but dies after the child's birth. Jerry and Michael must then bring up the child, also named Nellie and also played by Garland, despite their conflicts. Nellie soon falls in love with the wealthy Dennis Fogarty (Douglas McPhail), with her father's approval, but under her grandfather's protests, as he knew Fogarty's father (Arthur

The Films of Judy Garland

Shields) back in Ireland. Naturally, in the MGM tradition, all is wrapped up nicely at the end with everyone getting along with each other.

With unrest overseas that threatened to make its way to American shores, moviegoers throughout the nation longed for the sort of pleasant escapist fare offered by *Little Nellie Kelly* after enduring the ravages of the Depression. And for Judy Garland, playing a grownup who marries, has a child, and dies was a real transition. Some critics were as unsettled as studio head Louis B. Mayer, indicating they weren't ready to see her get married. Others said that Garland got prettier in each subsequent film, and all praised her singing and acting. Once she begins playing the daughter of her earlier character, Garland settles comfortably in a role that is more similar to the characters she had been playing.

Garland is really quite magnificent in the early scenes, where she must employ an effective Irish accent, perform a heartbreaking death scene, and receive her first real screen kiss. Her death scene was so powerful that crew members left the set so as not to be caught on the

Douglas McPhail and Judy Garland in *Little Nellie Kelly*, in which Garland plays her first adult role.

The Early Years—*Little Nellie Kelly* (1940)

soundtrack crying. One of Garland's sisters was also visiting that day, and she couldn't even watch them film the scene. It would be the only death scene Garland would play in her motion picture career. Hedda Hopper stated in her column:

> In the first part of *Little Nellie Kelly*, Judy Garland plays her own mother. That sequence ends with a death scene, then picks up again with Judy as her own daughter. The morning the death scene was to be done, Judy said to director Norman Taurog, I sort of dread this. I hate to die because I've grown to love this character. That's a wonderful sign, Taurog continued. The fact that Judy had a highly personalized feeling toward the character shows how talented she is.[30]

These early scenes exhibited Garland's range as an actress and proved to MGM that she was quite capable of starring in her own films.

The scenes in which George Murphy (who was 20 years older than Garland) plays her husband might seem off kilter, but that is only to balance out the fact that Murphy also plays her father for the better part of the movie. Murphy had appeared with Garland in *Broadway Melody of 1938* and was already something of a screen veteran by this time, as well as a former Broadway performer. He would work with Garland again

Garland plays nicely opposite Douglas McPhail, in one of only a few films where the young man got enough screen time to register. He had appeared with Garland and Mickey Rooney in *Babes in Arms* opposite Betty Jaynes, whom he would later marry. But despite showing some promise, MGM had hired him as another Nelson Eddy, not realizing that the classical style which suited McPhail's voice would fall out of favor by the late 1930s and be replaced by the swinging jazz style that he didn't effectively perform. McPhail committed suicide in 1944.

Charles Winninger had played Mickey Rooney's old vaudevillian father in *Babes in Arms*, would play Judy Garland's old vaudevillian father in her next movie, *Ziegfeld Girl*, and might be best known, due to constant reruns, for playing the old vaudeville partner of Fred Mertz (William Frawley) on TV's *I Love Lucy* some years later. And, in real life, Winninger was, indeed, an old vaudevillian. Winninger is delightfully blustery in a rather comical manner throughout the movie, but has one especially powerful dramatic moment. As he staggers weeping from the hospital room where his daughter just died, he is shown his new baby granddaughter and his sobs turn to a teary-eyed smile. Winninger pulls this off very effectively.

Director Norman Taurog's career dated back to the silent comedies of Larry Semon and would extend into several 1950s Martin and

The Films of Judy Garland

Lewis comedies and 1960s Elvis Presley movies, with such classics as *The Adventures of Tom Sawyer* and *Boys Town* along the way. This was Taurog's first chance to direct an Arthur Freed production. He would direct Judy Garland again.

As stated, critical opinion was mixed regarding *Little Nellie Kelly*, especially the idea of 18-year-old Garland playing an adult role for part of the movie. *Film Daily* stated in its review:

> Miss Garland sings pleasingly and puts her numbers over with a great deal of charm and appeal in addition to doing a nice bit of acting where it is demanded. It may seem incongruous to some people, however, to see Miss Garland get married, have a baby and die in the early sequences of the picture.[31]

John Scott's review in the *Los Angeles Times* felt the movie dragged in parts and also reacted to Garland playing an adult role:

> Judy Garland now joins the grown-ups on the screen. She plays both Nellie Kelly and Little Nellie Kelly, mother and daughter, respectively, in the film version of George M. Cohan's musical comedy. It is difficult to imagine the youthful Miss Garland in a wife and mother role, but then we'll just dismiss it with a slow shake of the head and a muttered, "Guess we're all getting on." The singing actress, who gains star billing in Little Nellie Kelly gives a very fine performance. And just a few years ago, she was only a child (there we go again). The picture is too long in this reviewer's opinion. Early scenes with an Ireland locale, showing the courtship of Nellie, Jerry Kelly (George Murphy) over papa's (Charles Winninger) objections, seem drawn out. Eventually the Kellys and father (Winninger) arrive in America. Nellie dies in child birth, papa and grandpapa continue their feud, and finally Little Nellie grows up as the image of her mother. There's a young man (Douglas McPhail) who wants to court Little Nellie, but grandfather again objects. He's straightened out, however, gets a job and everything ends happily. Incidentally, Murphy has worked his way up from a subway guard to a captain of police. Highlights of the picture are songs by Miss Garland, including "Nellie Kelly I Love You," "Singin' in the Rain" and other familiar ditties. Norman Taurog's direction is at a leisurely tempo. Murphy pleases and Winninger has a field day as grandpop.[32]

Theater owners in the trades, however, indicated that their patrons were quite satisfied with the movie, stating, "This is a sweet little picture and this picture had appeal for everyone. Judy Garland turns in a fine performance."[33]

One fan wrote into the trades herself to express how a viewing of *Little Nellie Kelly* at her local theater affected her:

> I just had a good cry. I saw *Little Nellie Kelly* and I didn't have a handkerchief either. I thought that Judy Garland was stepping out of her class when I heard she was falling in love and having a baby in the movie. I really wasn't

The Early Years—*Ziegfeld Girl* (1941)

expecting anything like I saw in *Little Nellie Kelly*. Here's hoping for many more just like *Little Nellie Kelly*.[34]

It was the moviegoers that mattered most to the studio. *Little Nellie Kelly* was a box office hit, and Judy Garland's motion picture career continued to advance.

Shortly after completing production on *Little Nellie Kelly*, Garland entered the hospital for a tonsillectomy. There was some apprehension because she had been putting it off for some time and her tonsils were seriously inflamed. This, plus the fact that she was still a teenager, made it possible that her voice could be affected by the operation. Fortunately, that did not happen.

Ziegfeld Girl

Directed by Robert Z. Leonard
Musical numbers directed by Busby Berkeley
Screenplay by Marguerite Roberts and Sonya Leven (from a story by William Anthony McGuire)
Produced by Pandro S. Berman
Cinematography by Ray June
Film editing by Blanche Sewell
Songs:
"You Never Looked So Beautiful"; Music by Walter Donaldson; Lyrics by Harold Adamson
"Minnie from Trinidad"; Written by Roger Edens
"I'm Always Chasing Rainbows"; Music by Harry Carroll; Lyrics by Joseph McCarthy
"Laugh? I Thought I'd Split My Sides"; Written by Roger Edens
"You Stepped Out of a Dream"; Music by Nacio Herb Brown; Lyrics by Gus Kahn
"Caribbean Love Song"; Music by Roger Edens; Lyrics by Ralph Freed
"Mr. Gallagher and Mr. Shean"; Written by Edward Gallagher and Al Shean
"Ziegfeld Girls"; Written by Roger Edens
"You Gotta Pull Strings"; Music by Walter Donaldson; Lyrics by Harold Adamson

The Films of Judy Garland

Cast: James Stewart, Judy Garland, Hedy Lamarr, Lana Turner, Tony Martin, Jackie Cooper, Ian Hunter, Charles Winninger, Edward Everett Horton, Phillip Dorn, Paul Kelly, Eve Arden, Dan Dailey, Al Shean, Fay Holden, Felix Bressart, Rose Hobart, Bernard Nedell, Ed McNamara, Mae Busch, Renie Riano, Josephine Whittell, Sergio Orta, Joyce Compton, James Flavin, George Lloyd, Reed Hadley, Eddie Hall, Armand Kaliz, Ruth Tobey, Gayne Whitman, John Alban, Jimmy Ames, King Baggott, Joan Barclay, James Conaty, Bess Flowers, Al Hill, Elliot Sullivan, Phil Morris, Colin Kenny, Donald Kirke, George Nolsom, Barry Norton, Anne O'Neal, Ginger Pearson, Ray Teal, Betty Allen, Tex Brodus, Bill Days, Alva Kellogg, Lois Lindsay, Rose Paidar, Helen Peterson, John Rarig, Virginia Rees, Max Smith, Christine Stafford, Irma Wilson, Victoria Vinton, Jean Wallace, Dorothy Tuttle, Anya Tranda, Amzie Strickland, Harriet Bennet, Nina Bissell, Leslie Brooks, Georgia Carroll, Virginia Cruzon, Patricia Dane, Myrna Dell, Frances Gladwin, Claire James, Louise La Planche, Madeline Martin, Vivian Mason, Rebel Randall, Dorothy Raye, and the Music Maids
Released April 25, 1941
Metro-Goldwyn-Mayer
132 Minutes
Black and White

MGM produced the Oscar winner for Best Picture, *The Great Ziegfeld*, in 1936, and had planned *Ziegfeld Girl* to be a sequel as early as 1938. A blurb in Louella Parsons' column in April of that year stated that Paulette Goddard, then Charlie Chaplin's wife, was being considered for such a film. Other than some bit roles, Goddard's only screen appearance at the time was Chaplin's *Modern Times* in 1936. Her 1938 movies *The Young in Heart* and *Dramatic School* hadn't yet been released. Parsons announced:

> Charlie Chaplin has returned, after a three-month sojourn at Pebble Beach, to his mansion atop the hill, joining Paulette Goddard there for the first time since she returned from Florida. Paulette, for a girl who made only one picture, and a silent one at that, has had a lot of publicity, and soon we shall see whether her talents deserve the break the producers give her, or whether she is another one of these girls whose ballyhoo overshadows her ability. We speak of Paulette particularly this morning because William Anthony McGuire has written *Ziegfeld Girl* with her in mind. She started with Ziegfeld in the chorus before she made her debut in the movies as a Goldwyn girl.[35]

The Early Years—*Ziegfeld Girl* (1941)

By July 1938, the press announced that Joan Crawford, Margaret Sullavan, Virginia Bruce, and Eleanor Powell would portray the four main Ziegfeld girls when William Anthony McGuire put *Ziegfeld Girl* in production.[36] And in 1939, the cast as we know it started to form with both Lana Turner and Hedy Lamarr announced. Lamarr even commented that she felt miscast:

> Serious doubts were expressed by Hedy Lamarr that she actually was being considered for *Ziegfeld Girl*. I shouldn't play an American girl, she told me. I couldn't do it any more than an American girl could play a continental. The first time in my life I've ever heard a foreign actress that frank and sensible. But Hedy might like to know that the part she is to play in *Ziegfeld Girl* permits her accent, and she will be seen with Lana Turner as the other glamour chorine. Margaret Sullavan has the dramatic spot and Mack Gordon and Harry Warren are writing the music.[37]

However, at the dawn of the 1940s, *Ziegfeld Girl* still hadn't been put into production. When it finally was, Mervyn LeRoy was not the producer as previously announced, and Mack Gordon and Harry Warren did not compose the music.

Even after *Ziegfeld Girl* was ready for production, Judy Garland wasn't originally supposed to be in the movie at all. It was going to star James Stewart, Hedy Lamarr, Eleanor Powell, and Lana Turner. However, Eleanor Powell became ill and wasn't able to be in the movie. At first, the press announced that MGM was considering Ann Miller to replace her:

> There's just a hint in the air that in case Eleanor Powell does not fully recuperate for some time from her illness, it may be Ann Miller who will be seen as the dancing star of Ziegfeld Girl. However, the studio would be inclined to stretch the starting date past the usual limits to retain Miss Powell. Nevertheless, Miss Miller is being importantly considered for dancing roles those days, since her success in the George White Scandals which led to her contract at R.K.O. for Too Many Girls.[38]

The studio then considered further and planned to further delay production on *Ziegfeld Girl* until Powell recuperated. The press announced that, in the meantime, they were putting Lana Turner in another project:

> It's more than probable that *Ziegfeld Girl* will be held in abeyance for a time at MGM due to delays in getting the cast together because some are otherwise occupied. Wherefore Lana Turner, slated for the picture, will be doing *Presenting Lily Mars*, which promises to be quite a stout dramatic subject for this young lady since Booth Tarkington wrote the novel. Pandro Berman will

produce the picture, pertaining to a smalltown girl who becomes a celebrated actress. Lana will be back from Honolulu this week to start preparations.³⁹

Ironically, not only was it *Presenting Lily Mars* that was put on hold; production commenced on *Ziegfeld Girl* with Judy Garland replacing Eleanor Powell, and Garland also ended up starring in *Presenting Lily Mars* when it began production a couple years later.

Judy Garland felt inferior to Lana Turner and Hedy Lamarr, despite her enormous talent.

The Early Years—*Ziegfeld Girl* (1941)

The Ziegfeld Follies were in production annually from the 1900s until just after the 1930s. Ziegfeld died in 1932. Thus, *Ziegfeld Girl* is set in the 1920s. MGM wanted to have some level of authenticity, so it hired Al Shean of the vaudeville team Gallagher and Shean to appear as himself and do some bits from his old act with the actor who played Judy Garland's father, whose character is called Gallagher. Shean's actual partner, Ed Gallagher, had died in 1929. Originally, Frank Morgan was cast in the role, but he was replaced by actual vaudevillian Charles Winninger, who had just appeared with Garland in *Little Nellie Kelly*. It was suspected that Winninger would respond to the rhythm and cadence of the old Gallagher and Shean material more effectively.

MGM also sought to hire some dancers to appear in the chorus as Ziegfeld Girls. This wasn't difficult, as Ziegfeld clubs of woman dancers had sprung up throughout the nation. An article stated:

> It's seldom that Metro-Goldwyn-Mayer has indulged in a beauty quest, but *Ziegfeld Girl* is to inspire that procedure because the studio will select 12 pulchritudinous damsels to take part as the glorified charmers needed for the production. However, the studio makes known that this is not simply an ordinary beauty competition. The young ladies must have personality and acting ability as well, such as caused Mae Murray, Ann Pennington, Marilyn Miller, Lilyan Tashman and others to be chosen for special assignments in the Ziegfeld days. The search is to be instituted first in Hollywood and then carried afield if it is not entirely successful here.[40]

Ziegfeld Girl is a loosely episodic musical drama with an excellent cast, often turning in fine performances. Thus, it is not a Judy Garland movie, but it is a high profile, top level MGM release, and her contribution is formidable.

Garland plays Susan Gallagher, one of three young women who are chosen to be Ziegfeld Girls in the showman's latest follies. The others are Sandra Kolter (Hedy Lamarr) and Sheila Regan (Lana Turner). Susan is an innately talented seventeen-year-old whose father (Charles Winninger) was quite a star in vaudeville, and while he is still performing, his ideas are out of date. Her dad is getting on in years and she worries about him touring alone, so Susan convinces the producers to give him and his old partner a part in the show. They put him on first, expecting his old-fashioned style to bomb, which will keep him from continuing with the show.

While Garland's portion of the story about Susan and her father is interesting, it is overshadowed by the more dramatic episodes featuring Hedy Lamarr and Lana Turner. Sandra is a beautiful European woman touring with her husband, a violinist. While her husband is too sophisticated for the Follies, Sandra is given a job as a showgirl against his wishes. She becomes interested in a singer named Frank Merton (Tony Martin) but leaves him when it is discovered he is married, and reconciles with her husband. Sheila is an elevator operator with a boyfriend, Gil (James Stewart), who is a hard-working truck driver. She has big dreams, while Gil is comfortable as a blue-collar worker. She makes it into the Follies and refuses Gil's proposal of marriage. He then connects with a bootlegging racket and is sent to prison. Sheila becomes an alcoholic, which affects her performance, and she is fired from the Follies. Her life and her health begin to plummet, and Gil is privately told she isn't going to live. Still, she makes it to the latest Follies performance, but collapses once there. As Sandra and her husband rush to her aid, we hear Susan singing from the stage, now the star of the show.

Judy Garland has a pivotal role in *Ziegfeld Girl* and also a triumphant one, so it has some significance to the development of her screen career. But arguably, the story featuring Lana Turner is much more gripping. While Garland once again plays a girl who is family oriented, earnest, hardworking, and, ultimately, successful, it is Turner who gets the heaviest dramatic scene, and Turner who gets the melodrama. She also plays more specifically opposite to first-billed James Stewart, although Turner is billed below Judy Garland and Hedy Lamarr.

Furthermore, Hedy Lamarr's story—including themes of adultery—is also a much more mature and serious dramatic episode than Garland's segments where her vaudeville father tries to coach how she puts over a song, using outmoded methods that are ultimately scoffed at by producers. Perhaps there is a point to the more adult themes ending more unhappily—with Lamarr's character no longer in show business while Turner's character dies. The character Garland plays is the one who survives and achieves success in the Follies.

However, what emerges is parallel to what the film itself offers. Even though Garland's sub-plot is less dramatic, it is still engrossing in its own right. The character of Susan Gallagher is someone the audience can cheer on, as she exhibits hard work and determination along with a willingness to dispense with her own ambitions in order to support her has-been father. That she becomes ultimately successful is uplifting and inspiring, where the other characters make choices that range from unsettling to tragic. However, this film was important for Lana Turner, in that her performance showed her acting prowess and allowed her to transition from B pictures to A-level movies opposite the likes of

The Early Years—*Ziegfeld Girl* (1941)

Spencer Tracy, Clark Gable, and Robert Taylor. Her life would become tumultuous, but her career would remain strong.

James Stewart's top billing was for basically a supporting role, probably due to his Oscar-winning success in *The Philadelphia Story* demanding such a status. This was Stewart's last film before joining the military. He would not star in another movie until *It's a Wonderful Life* five years later. Judy Garland's pal and former beau Jackie Cooper exhibits why he was among the few Our Gang child actors to transition successfully to adult roles. His scene conveying the seriousness of Sheila's illness to Gil is heartbreakingly moving. Paul Kelly, best known for playing gangsters, shows another side of his ability as a Ziegfeld production assistant, teaming with the always delightfully amusing and eccentric Edward Everett Horton. Dan Dailey would later click as

Judy Garland was happy to work with old pal and former beau Jackie Cooper.

a movie song-and-dance man, but his career was just getting started when he appeared in *Ziegfeld Girl*. His performance as a rugged prizefighter with an eye on the downtrodden Sheila provides another layer of drama to her story.

Ziegfeld Girl was Pandro S. Berman's first MGM movie after having supervised many classic musicals at RKO featuring Fred Astaire and Ginger Rogers. It was a success at the box office, and Judy Garland received good notice from the press, but most of the attention went to the more compelling stories played by Lana Turner and Hedy Lamarr. Meanwhile, Garland herself continued to feel inferior to the striking beauty of her two actress co-stars, never realizing her own discernible beauty and enormous talent.

Hoping to again star in movie vehicles of her own and be allowed to grow up and play more adult roles like Lana Turner (who was only a year older), Garland discovered that MGM had other plans. She was assigned two more movies with Mickey Rooney—another Andy Hardy effort, and another backyard musical.

Life Begins for Andy Hardy

Produced and directed by George B. Seitz
Screenplay by Agnes Christine Johnston (based on characters created by Aurania Rouverol)
Cinematography by Lester White
Film editing by Elmo Vernon
Cast: Mickey Rooney, Judy Garland, Ray McDonald, Lewis Stone, Patricia Dane, Sara Haden, Fay Holden, George Breakston, Joseph Crehan, John Eldredge, Bess Flowers, Nora Lane, Tommy Kelly, Hollis Jewell, Sid Miller, Pierre Watkin, Purnell Pratt, Charlotte Wynters, Lester Matthews, Mira McKinney, Leonard Sues, George Ovey, and Byron Shores
The following actors were originally in the movie but their scenes were deleted: Ralph Byrd, Frank Ferguson, George M. Carleton, Manart Kippen, William Holmes, Gladden James, William Forrest Robert Winkler, Paul Newlan, and Duke York.
Released August 15, 1941
MGM

The Early Years—*Life Begins for Andy Hardy* (1941)

101 minutes
Black and White

In her last Andy Hardy appearance as Betsy Booth, Judy Garland is able to call upon her dramatic talents, because the film itself is much more serious and layered than the usual Hardy family movie. *Life Begins for Andy Hardy* has Andy, newly graduated from high school, choosing to spend the summer in New York City on his own. He wants to leave the trappings of his small town and get a temp job in the big city, with a desire to learn about the working world before attending college. Betsy Booth is a native New Yorker who understands the city, but small-town hick Andy continues to belittle her experience and efforts, loftily believing he'll not need anyone's help.

Andy shows up in the big city with some money, gets a room in a boarding house, and finds a job as an office boy. While at work, he is swept off his feet by the switchboard operator, who is clearly taking

Life Begins for Andy Hardy **reunited Judy with Mickey as Betsy Booth and Andy Hardy, but the story was much more serious.**

advantage of his homespun innocence. Andy finds Jimmy, a young man who longs to be a dancer in Broadway musicals, sleeping on a park bench, so he sneaks him up to his room. Andy comes home one night to find Jimmy dead on the floor, and fears the young man despondently committed suicide. He is relieved upon discovering that Jimmy actually had a heart defect and died of natural causes, but is still deeply distraught by the death itself.

Judy Garland's role is twofold. First, Betsy Booth is someone that Andy can confide in with his simple challenges, like having to stretch his money when he has to purchase things like food, soap, and other items that he never had to consider while living at home. He can also rely on her friendship when shaken by Jimmy's death. Finally, Betsy is far more worldly and sophisticated than Andy, despite his smug confidence, and realizes the switchboard operator is, as she describes, a "wolf-ess." Some simple sleuthing reveals the woman is married, albeit separated.

Andy Hardy quickly learns about the more challenging responsibilities that he never had to confront in Carvel, from the pressures of maintaining a job and budgeting his money, to marital infidelity, and even death. City-bred Betsy Booth, then, is the better person to appear opposite Andy, because the character is removed from his element and placed in an area that she understands better, despite her youth. The rest of the Hardy family has little to do, although Judge Hardy visits Andy in New York, sees the switchboard operator wink at him, and immediately realizes what's going on.

Although she was the only guest star of the Hardy Series to be billed above the title (further evidence of her growing stardom), Judy Garland was, certainly by that point, quite tired of playing juveniles. Curiously, she recorded several songs for this movie, including Cole Porter's "Easy to Love," "America My Country 'Tis of Thee," "Abide with Me" and "The Rosary," but none appear in the movie. Because two of these numbers are religious ones, it is quite probable that a funeral scene for Jimmy was planned for the film, but jettisoned during production.

It's quite odd that Garland doesn't sing in this movie outside of a brief rendition of "Happy Birthday." But she has some really great scenes with Rooney and some strong dialogue. Each of her appearances in this series further proves that the character of Betsy Booth is not the naïve child Andy perceives her to be, but this becomes especially noteworthy in this film. Betsy has somehow managed to retain a certain homespun manner, despite living in New York City, and is aware of things that naïve Andy doesn't consider. She projects innocence, but she is both

The Early Years—*Babes on Broadway* (1941)

savvy and wary of her surroundings. Andy is forced to learn, through painful experience, that life outside of the protective trappings of his small town can be dangerous, even tragic. Betsy is already aware of this. This dynamic effectively adds greater depth to the Betsy Booth character, just as the film itself stretches beyond the parameters of the usual Andy Hardy movie.

Judy Garland filmed her scenes for *Life Begins for Andy Hardy* between April and May of 1941 just as she started work on her next movie, *Babes on Broadway*, which was another backyard musical with Mickey Rooney. It was also in May 1941 when 19-year-old Garland announced her engagement to David Rose.

Babes on Broadway

Directed by Busby Berkeley
Screenplay by Fred Finklehoffe, Elaine Ryan (based on a story by Finklehoffe)
Produced by Arthur Freed
Cinematography by Lester White
Film editing by Fredrick Smyth
Songs:
  "Babes on Broadway"; Music by Burton Lane; Lyrics by E.Y. Harburg
  "How About You?"; Music by Burton Lane; Lyrics by Ralph Freed
  "Anything Can Happen in New York"; Music by Burton Lane; Lyrics by Ralph Freed
  "Hoe Down"; Music by Roger Edens; Lyrics by Ralph Freed
  "Chin Up, Cheerio, Carry On"; Music by Burton Lane; Lyrics by E.Y. Harburg
  "Mary's a Grand Old Name"; Written by George M. Cohan
  "She Is Ma Daisy"; Music by Harry Lauder; Lyrics by Harry Lauder and J.D. Harper
  "I've Got Rings on My Fingers"; Music by Maurice Scott; Lyrics by Fred J. Barnes and R.P. Weston
  "The Yankee Doodle Boy"; Written by George M. Cohan
  "Bombshell from Brazil"; Written by Roger Edens
  "Mamãe Eu Quero"; Written by Jararaca and Vicente Paiva

The Films of Judy Garland

"By the Light of the Silvery Moon"; Music by Gus Edwards; Lyrics by Edward Madden
"Franklin D. Roosevelt Jones"; Written by Harold Rome
"Waiting for the Robert E. Lee"; Music by Lewis F. Muir; Lyrics by L. Wolfe Gilbert
Cast: Mickey Rooney, Judy Garland, Fay Bainter, Virginia Weidler, Ray McDonald, Richard Quine, Donald Meek, Alexander Woollcott, James Gleason, Donna Reed, Joe Yule, Margaret O'Brien, Luis Alberni, Emma Dunn, Fredrick Burton, Cliff Clark, William Post, Jr., Barbara Bedford, Lester Dorr, Bryant Washburn, Sidney Miller, Anne Rooney, Roger Steele, William A. Lee, Jean Porter, Jack "Tiny" Lipson, Six Hits and a Miss, The Debutantes, The Notables, The Peter Brothers, The Stafford Quartet, and Stop Look and Listen Trio
Released December 31, 1941
MGM
118 minutes
Black and White

Something of an extension of *Babes in Arms*, but not a sequel, *Babes on Broadway* has Mickey Rooney, Judy Garland, and some talented friends putting on a Broadway show to benefit an orphanage. They entertain at a block party to raise funds to rent an old rundown theater, but the building is condemned just as they are about to give their show. In an unsettling development, Rooney's character is presented as having no real interest in helping the orphanage—he is just using the situation to get on Broadway. Just as in their other musicals, Rooney and Garland start out as friends, become a couple, have conflicts, and make up at the end.

It is interesting that screenwriter Fred Finklehoffe decided to show a selfish, cynical side to the Rooney character, breaking away from the homespun wholesomeness and energetic scrupulousness he exhibited in the other Rooney-Garland musicals and the Andy Hardy series. And while her talent shines in these films, Judy Garland is essentially just responding to Mickey Rooney. It is his character that is most central to the narrative.

However, it is important to note that Rooney pursues Garland in this movie, not the other way around. She doesn't long for him, or pine for him. She doesn't sing a song about her crush on him. She is actually quite independent, especially for the era. It is also interesting that the relationship between the Rooney and Garland characters wasn't already

The Early Years—*Babes on Broadway* (1941)

Mickey Rooney and Judy Garland, together again, in *Babes on Broadway*.

established at the start of the film. They meet a bit into the film, and realize over the course of the movie that they have a good dynamic and a special connection—their performance of "How About You?" solidifies this.

Babes on Broadway went into production right around the time Shirley Temple was hired by MGM. She was originally set to appear in the film, but her mother refused, realizing she'd be overshadowed by Rooney and Garland. Her role went to another child star who was approaching adolescence, Virginia Weidler.

Because *Babes on Broadway* had an original screenplay, producer Arthur Freed wanted an original score. He hired songwriters Burton Lane, Yip Harburg, and Ralph Freed to compose songs that responded to the screenplay and characters appropriately so there would be an organic connection.

Judy Garland continued to have conflicts with Busby Berkeley's method of direction, but the musical numbers, which carry the film, are brilliantly staged. Berkeley's camera placement and choice of shots help to enhance the songs and dances.

The Films of Judy Garland

Babes on Broadway has become a rather unsettling film to enjoy in the 21st century due to a blackface number that is one of the major numbers in the production. In a book on Mickey Rooney's films, this writer stated:

> A lengthy minstrel sequence, complete with blackface makeup and broad dialect, is unsettling to see in the 21st century, but it has some level of historical/cultural significance in that the filmmakers and performers had no interest in being derogatory or insulting. Perhaps this can be considered ignorance, and it is an issue that should have more discussion than space will allow in a chapter such as this. But such acts were indeed a part of show business at one time, and that they are captured on film gives us a sociocultural checkpoint to inspire further study. This is not to defend or excuse its presentation, of course, but to defend our right to see it and respond to it during these more enlightened times.[41]

During the filming of *Babes on Broadway,* 19-year-old Judy Garland flew to Las Vegas and eloped with David Rose. Louis B. Mayer was upset that she eloped rather than allowing the studio to garner publicity with a big wedding, and refused to give Garland a honeymoon. She was ordered to report back to the set the next day. Meanwhile, Mickey Rooney met his future first wife Ava Gardner while filming *Babes on Broadway,* when the attractive young lady visited the set.

Babes on Broadway had a very high (for the time) budget of $955,000, but it was an enormous hit, earning nearly four million dollars. Thomas Pryor writes in the *New York Times*:

> When Metro spreads itself on a production number, it invariably does a handsome job. And, it has done right nicely by the finale of *Babes on Broadway,* providing a mammoth eye-filling setting for the minstrel show which is the only racy and really entertaining episode in this otherwise dull and overly-long potpourri of comedy, drama, third-rate jokes and music. The humor department reached its zenith with the remark, "I'm going out to get some air, I feel rather flat," which Mickey Rooney tosses off rather sheepishly. As the title of the Music Hall's new offering implies, it is basically a story about the youngsters who hang out in the Times Square theatrical precincts, hoping for that one break which will open the gates to the pearly highway of the show world. You can observe, any day in the week, dozens of youngsters like those portrayed by Mickey Rooney and Judy Garland, congregating on the corners of Forty-fourth and Forty-fifth Streets and swapping tales of their experiences in trying to see this producer or that one. It's a sight familiar to most New Yorkers, and out of it some enterprising showman may yet evolve an entertaining musical edition of *Stage Door*. But Metro, with Mr. Rooney on its hands, just couldn't follow a simple straightforward story line. So, except

The Early Years—*For Me and My Gal* (1942)

for an occasional and pleasant musical interruption by Miss Garland, the plot is thickened with some trite nonsense about Mickey and Judy staging a settlement house show to raise funds to send some underprivileged children to the country. As usual, Mickey Rooney does not confine himself to a single characterization, but gives also his impersonations of Sir Harry Lauder very bad, George M. Cohan fair, a hillbilly idiot exaggerated but amusing and a black-faced end man lively and in the best Elks Club tradition. Though Mickey doesn't leave much room for anybody else, Judy Garland manages to stand out in the musical interludes, as does the graceful and nimble-footed Ray McDonald in a brief tap dance.[42]

While Garland is mentioned, Rooney dominates the review, as he did most others. Garland loved Rooney, but realized it was time to move out of his shadow.

Just as she was beginning to transition to more adult roles, *Babes on Broadway* was something of a step back for Judy Garland, despite its popularity with moviegoers. Doing a death scene a couple of films earlier and starting to play a woman with some level of independence wasn't quite enough for MGM to realize it was time for Garland to grow up and remain an adult in her subsequent movies. But that was finally proven with her next movie.

For Me and My Gal

Directed by Busby Berkeley
Screenplay by Richard Sherman, Fred Finklehoffe, and Sid Silvers
  (based on a story by Howard Emmett Rogers)
Produced by Arthur Freed
Cinematography by William H. Daniels
Film editing by Ben Lewis
Songs:
  "For Me and My Gal"; Music by George W. Meyer; Lyrics by
    Edgar Leslie and E. Ray Goetz
  "Oh Johnny, Oh Johnny Oh!"; Music by Abe Olman
  "The Doll Shop"; Music and Lyrics by Roger Edens
  "Oh, You Beautiful Doll"; Music by Nat Ayer; Lyrics by A. Seymour Brown
  "Don't Leave Me Daddy"; Written by Joseph M. Verges
  "The Oceana Roll"; Music by Lucien Denni

The Films of Judy Garland

"By the Beautiful Sea"; Music by Harry Carroll; Lyrics by Harold Atteridge

"When You Wore a Tulip and I Wore a Big Red Rose"; Music by Percy Wenrich; Lyrics by Jack Mahoney

"They Go Wild Simply Wild Over Me"; Music by Fred Fisher; Lyrics by Joseph McCarthy

"Do I Love You?"; Music by E. Ray Goetz and Henri Christiné; Lyrics by E. Ray Goetz

"After You've Gone"; Music by Turner Layton; Lyrics by Henry Creamer

"The Sidewalks of New York"; Music by Charles Lawlor

"Some of These Days"; Music by Shelton Brooks

"Tell Me"; Music by Max Kortlander; Lyrics by J. Will Callahan

"Till We Meet Again"; Music by Richard A. Whiting; Lyrics by Ray Egan

"We Don't Want the Bacon What We Want Is a Piece of the Rhine!"; Written by Howard Carr, Harry Russell, and Jimmie Havens

"Ballin' the Jack"; Music by Chris Smith; Lyrics by Jim Burris

"What Are You Going to Do to Help the Boys?"; Music by Egbert Van Alstyne; Lyrics by Gus Kahn

"Goodbye Broadway, Hello France"; Music by Billy Baskette; Lyrics by C. Francis Reisner and Benny Davis

"Hinky Dinky Parlay Voo Mad'moiselle from Armentières"; Music by Irwin Dash; Lyrics by Al Dubin and Joe Mittenthal

"How 'Ya Gonna Keep 'em Down on the Farm After They've Seen Paree?"; Music by Walter Donaldson; Lyrics by Sam Lewis and Joe Young

"There's a Long, Long Trail"; Music by Zo Elliott; Lyrics by Stoddard King

"Where Do We Go from Here?"; Written by Percy Wenrich and Howard Johnson

"It's a Long, Long Way to Tipperary"; Written by Jack Judge and Harry Williams

"Smiles"; Music by Lee S. Roberts; Lyrics by J. Will Callahan

"Oh Frenchy"; Music by Con Conrad; Lyrics by Sam Ehrlich

"Pack Up Your Troubles"; Music by Felix Powell; Lyrics by George Asaf

"When Johnny Comes Marching Home"; Written by Louis Lambert

Cast: Judy Garland, George Murphy, Gene Kelly, Martha Eggerth, Ben Blue, Stephen McNally, Richard Quine, Lucille Norman,

The Early Years—*For Me and My Gal* (1942)

Edward Peil, Sr., Keenan Wynn, Libby Taylor, Joe Yule, Walter Baldwin, John Dilson, Rad Robinson, Gladden James, Nestor Paiva, Shep Houghton, Al Hill, Robert Homans, Hooper Atchley, Gurney Bell, Bill Days, Jay Meyer, Jay Moffitt, Ken Darby, John Dodson, Mickey Golden, Ruth Dwyer, John Breen, George Davis, Lester Dorr, Addison Richards, Ben Lessey, Harry Rosenthal, William Tannen, Anne Rooney, and John Breen
Released October 21, 1942
MGM
104 minutes
Black and White

For Me and My Gal is important not only for being the first full adult role for Judy Garland, but also for being Gene Kelly's debut. The concept started out as far back as 1940, when producer Arthur Freed considered making a film that recalled Judy Garland's stage roots. MGM bought the screen rights to the Howard Emmett Rogers story *The Big Time*, which was a nostalgic look back at vaudeville.

Originally the film was going to feature two female leads and two male leads, one a singer and the other a dancer. Eleanor Powell and Dan Dailey were considered, but that changed when Dailey was drafted. It was Broadway actress Stella Adler, now an assistant producer at MGM who then suggested the two female roles be combined into one, to be played by Judy Garland. That would create a love triangle between the two male leads. George Murphy, who had worked well with Garland in the recent *Little Nellie Kelly*, was given the more important male lead of Harry Palmer. However, things changed when Judy Garland attended a Broadway show. According to Louella Parsons:

> When Judy Garland was in New York she saw Pal Joey and then went around sounding like a press agent about young Gene Kelly. When she came back home, she kept on raving about how wonderful he would be for pictures. Apparently, her MGM bosses have decided that Judy is an A-l talent scout for not only have they signed him on a term contract but Gene is handed to Judy for the male lead opposite her in The Big Time. This song and dance story about the good old days of vaudeville gets going right away at Culver City with Arthur Freed as producer.[43]

Gene Kelly had been signed by David O. Selznick, who didn't have any film work for him. A year had passed with still no work for Kelly from Selznick, so Arthur Freed requested Kelly's services for *The Big Time*. An agreement was made and Kelly was put into the role of Harry

Palmer. This meant that George Murphy was relegated to the smaller male lead, much to his chagrin.

Judy Garland stars as Jo Hayden, a vaudeville singer-dancer in a troupe run by Jimmy Metcalf (George Murphy). Jo has a brother (Richard Quine) in college studying to be a doctor, but as America enters

Gene Kelly made his screen debut at Judy Garland's request in *For Me and My Gal.*

The Early Years—*For Me and My Gal* (1942)

World War I he is drafted. Harry Palmer (Gene Kelly) is a brash vaudeville song-and-dance man whose talent is formidable but whose ego surpasses that. He is charismatic enough to entice Jo to join his act, and Jimmy makes the sacrifice because he is secretly in love with Jo. Jo, meanwhile, is in love with Harry, who is too focused on the act. In fact, at a Chicago gig, another entertainer, Eve Minard (Marta Eggerth), tries to tell Jo that Harry is an opportunist not worth her affection, and even stages a scene where Jo hides while Eve asks Harry to join her act. Harry barely hesitates before agreeing to do so. Then, when Harry is drafted, it seems that their act will not be able to continue, but on the very day that a heartbroken Jo receives a telegram indicating her brother has been killed in action, she discovers Harry has purposely disfigured his own hand to avoid the draft. Jo angrily rejects Harry, who feels remorseful. To make it up to her, he enlists despite his disability and entertains front-line troops. Harry performs a heroic act by warning an ambulance that it is heading to an impending ambush, and gets a commendation. After the war, Harry goes to the Palace Theater, where Jo is performing. She spots him in the audience and brings him on stage to sing a number with her.

The title of *The Big Time* was changed twice during production. The press referred to it simply as *Me and My Gal* in several articles while it was being filmed, but by the time it was released, it was called *For Me and My Gal*. According to producer Arthur Freed:

> I was trying to find a title from a song and I could have picked half a dozen songs as titles, but Edgar Leslie and George Mayer were friends of mine and I liked what they wrote, so I bought the rights to "For Me and My Gal" from Mills music Publishing Company for use of the title and song, and it became a standard.[44]

Judy Garland and Gene Kelly got along well during the filming of *For Me and My Gal*, especially due to the fact that Kelly challenged the ideas of director Busby Berkeley, whom Garland never liked. Because Kelly was so new to movies, he didn't have much clout to back up his objections, but Garland, a major star at the studio, supported him. Kelly never forgot the fact that Garland was so supportive and would repay this kindness later on when he was a star. Throughout the film, Garland assisted Kelly with his acting for the camera, having been a stage performer herself. Kelly had to adapt his broader gestures to more nuanced ones for the intimate movie camera. Judging by his performance, he did well. His lack of dancing in this movie is perhaps the most notable difference from his future films, but he handles the dramatic scenes effectively.

The Films of Judy Garland

After preview audiences disliked that Gene Kelly's character was a draft dodger, retakes were shot showing him in uniform, with Judy Garland in *For Me and My Gal*.

Preview audiences were unhappy with the Harry Palmer character being both a womanizer and a draft-dodger, and believed that George Murphy's character should have ended up with Jo. Louis B. Mayer ordered three weeks of retakes, angrily telling Murphy that he spoiled the movie by playing his character as being too nice of a guy. The retakes allowed the Harry Palmer character scenes in which he showed remorse for his actions, and also whittled down Murphy's role. The finale was originally supposed to feature all three actors, but in the final cut it was only Judy Garland and Gene Kelly. This further upset George Murphy, who was already angered by being removed from the Harry Palmer role and having to play, what he called, "the schnook who doesn't get the girl." He left MGM for RKO soon afterward.

In spite of the added scenes and Harry's redemption at the end, it's kind of shocking that MGM presented this type of character, especially in the midst of World War II. Harry still comes off as pretty despicable when he smashes his hand, despite being the film's main protagonist. The film still pulls off a pretty patriotic ending with a pro-enlistment message, but the approach to Kelly's character is still a bit surprising in context.

While his conflicts with both Gene Kelly and Judy Garland were unsettling, director Busby Berkeley would later cite this film as his favorite. Curiously, the film did not feature any of the director's noted overhead shots or kaleidoscope-styled musical numbers.

The Early Years—*Presenting Lily Mars* (1943)

For Me and My Gal was an enormous hit at the box office, securing stardom for Gene Kelly and showing MGM that 19-year-old Judy Garland would be accepted as a grownup. The film made nearly four times its production costs, which were formidable, as it was a major musical production, and was one of the biggest hits of the year. The critic for the *Los Angeles Daily News* was impressed overall, and noticed that George Murphy was relegated to mere support:

> The stars play a shoestring vaudeville team which dreams of the day a date at the Palace will come along. Of course it does, but not before the boy and girl have been through World War I as entertainers at the front and Kelly has had the opportunity to prove a hero. Nostalgic tunes of yesterday punctuate the piece and they're delightfully done. In fact, the picture is completely winning even if a little too long. Miss Garland has the faculty (wonderful for her but tough on an audience) of melting your heart, and in a sympathetic part she's murder. But when she cries, its practically your cue to follow unless you be of stern stuff. As for Kelly, he's glimpsed as a likable guy with heelish qualities who doesn't quite give in to them. He's a smooth performer, smooth as a singer, dancer and actor. Much can be expected of him in the future. *For Me and My Gal* means little for George Murphy, who is mainly shunted in the background as Miss Garland's faithful friend.[45]

For Me and My Gal was also a turning point for Judy Garland in that she would no longer be playing the young girl in pigtails or the Betsy Booth types. Not that these elements disappeared entirely and immediately. Despite the fact that it is obvious that she is playing an adult character here, it is still a character who spends half the film yearning for the leading man, who initially doesn't notice her in a romantic way. Garland also expressed an interest in doing some straight dramatic acting, playing more challenging roles that had layered character elements and greater depth. The studio eventually did take notice.

An evolution in Judy Garland's screen work was happening here and it would slowly evolve over her next several projects. Meanwhile, her personal life and substance abuse did not get any easier.

Presenting Lily Mars

Directed by Norman Taurog
Screenplay by Richard Connell and Gladys Lehman, with

contributions by Frances Marion and Jack Minz (from a novel by Booth Tarkington)
Produced by Joe Pasternak
Cinematography by Joseph Ruttenberg
Film editing by Albert Akst
Songs:
  "Tom, Tom, the Piper's Son"; Music by Burton Lane; Lyrics by E.Y. Harburg
  "Is It Really Love or the Gypsy in Me?"; Music by Walter Jurmann; Lyrics by Paul Francis Webster
  "Every Little Movement Has a Meaning All Its Own"; Music by Karl Hoschna; Lyrics by Otto A. Harbach
  "When I Look at You"; Music by Walter Jurmann; Lyrics by Paul Francis Webster
  "When You Think of Lovin', Baby Think of Me"; Written by Don Swander and June Hershey
  "Kulebiaka Russian Rhapsody"; Written by Paul Francis Webster and Walter Jurmann
  "Where There's Music"; Music and Lyrics by Roger Edens
  "Three O'Clock in the Morning"; Music by Julián Robledo; Lyrics by Dolly Morse
  "Broadway Rhythm"; Music by Nacio Herb Brown; Lyrics by Arthur Freed
Cast: Judy Garland, Van Heflin, Fay Bainter, Richard Carlson, Spring Byington, Martha Eggerth, Connie Gilchrist, Leonid Kinskey, Patricia Barker, Janet Chapman, Annie Ross, Douglas Croft, Ray McDonald, Tommy Dorsey, Bob Crosby, Bill Cartledge, Lynne Carver, Vicky Lane, Marilyn Maxwell, Lew Payton, Gus Schilling, Henry Sylvester, William Tannen, Lillian Yarbo, Joe Yule, Betty Blythe, Abigail Adams, Bobby Barber, Almira Sessions, Barbara Bedford, Eric Braunsteiner, Frank Coghlan, Jr., Judy Carol, Foncilla Adams, Bill Dill, Wally Cassell, Robert Cauterio, Jack Chefe, Helen Dickson, Al Murphy, Mary Elliot, Buddy Morrow, Virginia Gumm, Virginia Engels, Marcella Holmes, Alberto Mann, Mary Alice Moore, Carl Leviness, Charles Meakin, Claire McDowell, Remington Olmstead, Lee Murray, Lee and Lynn Wilde, Charles Walters, Jack Vlaskin, Bruce Squires, Harry Rosenthal, Max Herman, Pete Carpenter, and Ray Bauduc
Released April 29, 1943
MGM
104 minutes
Black and White

The Early Years—*Presenting Lily Mars* (1943)

As stated earlier in the text, the idea to film Booth Tarkington's *Presenting Lily Mars* was originally planned as a drama starring Lana Turner due to delays in the production of *Ziegfeld Girl*. However, when plans changed, this project was shelved. When it was resurrected for Judy Garland, it was revamped as a musical comedy while retaining the basic narrative and a lot of the dramatic elements.

Judy Garland was quite pleased with being cast in this film. Desiring to transition to adult roles, and wanting to explore her acting abilities more deeply, *Presenting Lily Mars* was just the type of project she sought. Garland also had a strong sense of humor and loved comedy, as one of her dearest friends was comedian Phil Silvers. So, she was further pleased with the idea that she'd have a chance to be funny. Finally, it was Garland's first film with producer Joe Pasternak, who had just come to MGM from Universal, where he had produced the movies that launched Deanna Durbin's career. Pasternak wanted to work with Garland, and she wanted to work with him.

George Murphy was originally going to play the theatrical producer who falls for Garland in the title role, but he had just left MGM for RKO. The studio then decided to cast Van Heflin in the role. Heflin had scored big in *Johnny Eager*, which had been released in January 1942. He was nominated for the Academy Award as Best Supporting Actor for a brilliant portrayal of a drunken gangster tortured by his feelings toward the title character, played by Robert Taylor. Heflin would win the Oscar at the 1943 ceremonies. While the character he played in *Johnny Eager* was a serious drama, Heflin had a real flair for comedy and settled very comfortably into his lighthearted role for this film.

Judy Garland plays 19-year-old Lily Mars, the eldest child of widow Spring Byington, who manages to support the family by making custom hats. One of those hats is for Mimi Thornway (Fay Bainter), whose son John (Van Heflin) is a top Broadway producer. Lily is talented, longs to appear on stage, and hopes that Mimi will put in a good word with John. Of course, John, who has had several talentless people thrust in front of him by well-meaning Mimi, will have none of it. Lily devises a series of schemes, from stealing his personal copy of his latest show's script, to staging a scene with her little sister at a window outside Mimi's house in full view of John and crashing the after party of his show. When she sings with the band, John is distracted, but remains cold. Lily claims John is suppressing an attraction to her, and goes home and sobs with her siblings. Lily's mother tells her to go to New York and follow her dream. She does so, but when she sneaks into John's show as a dancer,

Judy Garland worked well with her co-star Van Heflin in *Presenting Lily Mars*.

she collapses from hunger. John is sympathetic, and arranges a room for her at a boarding house. The two are at a nightclub when Lily gets on stage and mocks Isobel (Martha Eggerth), John's haughty leading lady with whom he has been romantically involved. Isobel comes to the nightclub unexpectedly, sees what Lily is doing, and leaves the show. Lily takes her place, but it is a bit too much for a beginner and she comes

The Early Years—*Presenting Lily Mars* (1943)

off poorly. John makes peace with Isobel, who returns to the play, and Lily returns to her small role, just as her family arrives in New York to see her starring debut. But Lily's determination and innate talent eventually make her a star.

This unconventional ending is effective. It feels much more realistic than Lily suddenly rocketing to stardom, but also still provides the satisfaction of the time jump at the finale showing that she did eventually become a star. It made this otherwise conventional-seeming movie unconventional.

While Judy Garland is still playing the daughter, her romance is with a man, and her problems in the narrative are those of an adult, not a child pretending to be an adult like in some of the early musicals with Mickey Rooney. This makes *Presenting Lily Mars* a transitional film, in that it led the way toward adult roles for Garland.

Garland may have been transitioning from kid to adult in films, but her personal life was fraught with very grownup problems. MGM continued to work her so hard that her substance abuse became more pronounced. Garland was still finishing work on *For Me and My Gal* when she was in rehearsals for *Presenting Lily Mars*. She did a musical number for the all-star MGM production *Thousands Cheer* while still active on *Presenting Lily Mars*. And she was already active on her next film, *Girl Crazy*, when called back to reshoot the final musical number for *Presenting Lily Mars*.

Production on *Presenting Lily Mars* concluded in November 1942. Originally, this film concluded with a musical finale that included the song "Paging Mr. Greenback." Louis B. Mayer was underwhelmed by this number and asked Joe Pasternak if he could assign producer Arthur Freed to reshoot the finale. Pasternak agreed (although it is unlikely that he had a choice), and a new finale was shot. Reportedly, Judy Garland spent three months working on it, while also shooting *Girl Crazy*, finally completing the new finale in February 1943. It is significant that Garland's dance partner in the re-shot finale is Charles Walters, who was just getting into choreography from his status as a chorus boy, and would become one of the studio's most important directors.

Despite the grueling schedule, Judy Garland enjoyed working on *Presenting Lily Mars*. She liked her first experience with Joe Pasternak, was comfortable with director Norman Taurog, with whom she had worked previously, and she liked co-star Van Heflin. Thus, the filming of this movie went along without incident, other than the re-shot finale that was decided upon completion. Garland does get a lot of opportunities to do comedy in this movie, and she's really funny, from the early scenes where her character is overacting, to when she impersonates Martha Eggerth's character in the club. These are augmented with sweet and dramatic moments between her and Connie Gilchrist,

After working often with Mickey Rooney, Judy Garland got to play a scene with Rooney's father, Joe Yule, in *Presenting Lily Mars*.

The Early Years—*Girl Crazy* (1943)

who plays someone older who has spent her entire career on the stage and encourages Lily when she is down. Judy Garland's appearance starting with this movie is markedly different from her previous films. She looks so much more glamorous, and her hair is styled in a more mature way. Her physical appearance in addition to the type of role she was playing makes it clear that she is an adult now.

Presenting Lily Mars is perfectly entertaining, especially now when approached as an older film from a bygone era. But critics of the time were unimpressed. The one strong review came from the *Los Angeles Citizen Evening News* which stated:

> Metro-Goldwyn-Mayer took an excellent screenplay based on a Booth Tarkington novel, cast Judy Garland in the top role and then surrounded her with some of the best acting ability, musical numbers and popular orchestras to turn out *Presenting Lily Mars*. It is a tuneful musical comedy number with plenty of oomph in the right places, a lot of good laughs, and some fine acting as well as exceptional singing.[46]

Presenting Lily Mars certainly isn't one of Judy Garland's truly great films, but it was an enormous box office hit. As a big budget musical for a top studio, *Presenting Lily Mars* grossed nearly triple its production costs at the box office.

Despite that during this time, in January 1943, Garland separated from first husband David Rose (they would divorce the following year), this was a comparatively successful period for the actress. However, her own insecurities were such that even a series of beautiful portraits that were shot after the completion of *Presenting Lily Mars* and before *Girl Crazy* were not enough to give Garland confidence in her appearance. Meanwhile, her movies continued to be huge box office hits.

Girl Crazy

Directed by Norman Taurog and Busby Berkeley
Screenplay by Fred F. Finklehoffe, Dorothy Kingsley, William Ludwig, and Sid Silvers (from a play by Guy Bolton and Jack McGowan)
Produced by Arthur Freed
Cinematography by William H. Daniels and Robert H. Planck
Film editing by Albert Akst

The Films of Judy Garland

Songs:
- "I Got Rhythm"; Music by George Gershwin; Lyrics by Ira Gershwin
- "Treat Me Rough"; Music by George Gershwin; Lyrics by Ira Gershwin
- "Could You Use Me?"; Music by George Gershwin; Lyrics by Ira Gershwin
- "Bidin' My Time"; Music by George Gershwin; Lyrics by Ira Gershwin
- "Embraceable You"; Music by George Gershwin; Lyrics by Ira Gershwin
- "But Not for Me"; Music by George Gershwin; Lyrics by Ira Gershwin
- "Fascinating Rhythm"; Music by George Gershwin; Lyrics by Ira Gershwin
- "Sam and Delilah"; Music by George Gershwin; Lyrics by Ira Gershwin
- "Happy Birthday to You"; Music by Mildred J. Hill; Lyrics by Patty S. Hill
- "Barbary Coast"; Music by George Gershwin; Lyrics by Ira Gershwin
- "Boy! What Love Has Done to Me!"; Music by George Gershwin; Lyrics by Ira Gershwin

Cast: Mickey Rooney, Judy Garland, Gil Stratton, Robert E. Strickland, Rags Ragland, June Allyson, Nancy Walker, Tommy Dorsey, Guy Kibbee, Frances Rafferty, Henry O'Neill, Howard Freeman, Irving Bacon, William Beaudine, Jr., Jess Lee Brooks, Dick Haymes, Peter Lawford, Jo Stafford, Christine Stafford, Clark Yocum, Six Hits and a Miss, Merry Maids, Pied Pipers, Tommy Dorsey's orchestra, Karin Booth, Hazel Brooks, Georgia Carroll, Inez Cooper, Linda Deane, Natalie Draper, Mary Jane French, Carole Gallagher, Karen Gaylord, Aileen Hailey, Virginia Hunter, Lois James, Aileen Morris, and Noreen Nash

Released November 26, 1943
MGM
99 minutes
Black and White

Girl Crazy, based on George and Ira Gershwin's hit 1930 Broadway show, was filmed at RKO studios in 1932 with the comedy team of Bert Wheeler and Bob Woolsey, emphasizing the humor more than the music. This film concentrates more on the music and the personalities

The Early Years—*Girl Crazy* (1943)

of its leads, Mickey Rooney and Judy Garland, who were being paired in a movie for the last time.

Mickey Rooney plays Danny Churchill, an irresponsible, pampered playboy whose father wants to curb his embarrassing activities, so he arranges for him to attend an all-male college out west. Ginger (Judy Garland) is the girl who delivers the mail, and Danny becomes smitten with her rather quickly. Thus, unlike other films in which Mickey Rooney and Judy Garland appear, it is Rooney's character Danny who longs for Garland, who gets to play the more aloof Ginger. Having trouble fitting into this more rustic environment, Danny is about to quit school when he hears it is about to be closed due to low enrollment. Of

Judy Garland co-starred with Mickey Rooney for the last time in *Girl Crazy*.

course, he and Ginger raise the necessary enrollment of 125 new freshmen by putting on a show.

It is fun to see this movie play with the conventions established by Garland and Rooney's previous screen pairings and the reversing of their roles in the relationship dynamic. It's immediately obvious when we meet Garland's Ginger fixing a car that she is much more capable than Danny. As a result, they have perhaps the strongest chemistry here out of all of their movies. There are a couple moments where they have such an easygoing back and forth and laugh with each other so affectionately that it feels less like acting and more like a peek at their real friendship.

It is interesting that Danny Churchill is the complete opposite of Andy Hardy. Whereas Andy was a small town boy with lofty ideas who found himself out of place in the big city in *Life Begins for Andy Hardy*, Danny is a wealthy playboy who can't connect with the more rural environment. And, once again, Garland plays the character who is comfortably settled in this lifestyle.

However, in keeping with the idea that it was time MGM's younger stars started to transition into more grownup roles, *Girl Crazy* is not about altruistic teenagers putting on a show in dad's barn. This time, Garland's and Rooney's characters are young adults in a college setting. The result is what some consider the best of the Garland-Rooney musicals.

Some of the humor is formulaic. Of course, city boy Danny tries to ride a horse for the first time, hanging on frantically while it jerks and bucks, and there are other instances where city-savvy Danny has trouble adapting to country life. Meanwhile, Ginger laughs derisively at this big-shot who can't spin his way out of these situations with a lot of fast talk. However, this makes the formula gags more effective. Judy Garland had a noticeably infectious laugh, and her merriment extends to the viewer in these otherwise predictable scenes.

Girl Crazy was another Arthur Freed production, but after shooting the movie's finale (which was filmed first), Busby Berkeley was replaced by Norman Taurog as director. Judy Garland was now a big enough star at MGM where she could have directors she didn't like removed from productions, and Garland never did like Busby Berkeley. According to Mickey Rooney:

> Judy was exhausted, and was already taking pills to stay awake, to go to sleep, when she was told she was too fat or too thin. She did it secretly. And Buzz was pushing us past our limits. So Judy had him taken off the picture and they brought in Norman Taurog who was a friend of both of ours.[47]

The Early Years—*Girl Crazy* (1943)

Production on *Girl Crazy* was shut down for a month while the transition from Berkeley to Taurog took place.

Garland held up production when she went back to Hollywood from the film's desert location, allegedly for a romantic tryst, and while the production was waiting for her return, a sudden dust storm ruined some of the equipment. The actors and production people were idle in their hotels, bored and tense, so they started drinking. It was days before Garland finally returned.

The supporting cast is highlighted by such welcome veterans as Rags Ragland and Nancy Walker, and an early appearance by a young June Allyson. And despite a grueling production in hot weather during some Palm Springs location filming, and a sandstorm that destroyed some equipment (the production had to wait while new material was shipped to the location), *Girl Crazy* is sustained by its brilliant Gershwin score and a lot of good natured fun.

As with *Presenting Lily Mars*, *Girl Crazy* also initially had a different ending. Originally, Garland and Rooney led a finale with the song "Embraceable You," once Danny proposed to Ginger. Instead, the film shows the new freshmen applying for enrollment, and they are all girls, indicating that the school is now going to be co-educational.

Critics and audiences alike were happy about *Girl Crazy*, with James Agee, the reviewer for *Time*, stating:

> As sung by actress Judy Garland, "Embraceable You" and "Bidin' My Time" become hits all over again and the new "But Not for Me" sounds like another. Her presence is open, cheerful, warming. If she were not so profitably good at her own game, she could obviously be a dramatic cinema actress with profit to all.[48]

Variety also praised Garland:

> Miss Garland is a nifty saleswoman of the numbers, right down to the overproduced "Rhythm" finale which was Busby Berkeley's special chore. Her "Embraceable You" delivery is a standout; ditto "Bidin' My Time" and "But Not for Me." She's also got two nice dancing sessions.[49]

Girl Crazy grossed nearly four times its production costs. And while it was right within a very strong period for Judy Garland, it was near the end of Mickey Rooney's superstardom. Once a number one box office star, Rooney would enlist in the army after filming *National Velvet* (1944). In fact, 1945 was the first year with no new Mickey Rooney movie release since the silent era. When he returned in 1946, Rooney spent the rest of his life trying to recapture his pre-war stardom. Judy

The Films of Judy Garland

Garland was about to appear in some of her best films, and have opportunities to tap into deeper layers of her talent as an actress.

Meet Me in St. Louis

Directed by Vincente Minnelli
Screenplay by Irving Brecher and Fred Finklehoffe (based on the novel by Sally Benson)
Produced by Arthur Freed
Cinematography by George J. Folsey
Film editing by Albert Akst
Songs:
  "The Trolley Song"; Written by Hugh Martin and Ralph Blane
  "The Boy Next Door"; Written by Hugh Martin and Ralph Blane
  "Skip to My Lou"; Written by Hugh Martin and Ralph Blane
  "Have Yourself a Merry Little Christmas"; Written by Hugh Martin and Ralph Blane
  "Meet Me in St. Louis, Louis"; Music by Kerry Mills; Lyrics by Andrew B. Sterling
  "I Was Drunk Last Night"; Composer unknown
  "Under the Bamboo Tree"; Music by J. Rosamond Johnson; Lyrics by Bob Cole
  "Over the Bannister"; Written by Hugh Martin and Ralph Blane
  "You and I"; Music by Nacio Herb Brown; Lyrics by Arthur Freed
  "Brighten the Corner Where You Are"; Written by Ina D. Ogdon and Charles Gabriel
Cast: Judy Garland, Margaret O'Brien, Mary Astor, Lucille Bremer, Leon Ames, Tom Drake, Marjorie Main, Harry Davenport, June Lockhart, Henry H. Daniels, Jr., Joan Carroll, Hugh Marlowe, Robert Sully, Chill Wills, Sidney Barnes, Darryl Hickman, Mayo Newhall, Donald Curtis, Buddy Gorman, Sam Harris, Belle Mitchell, Myron Tobias, Kenneth Wilson, William Smith, Sid Newman, Judi Blacque, Helen Gilbert, Charlotte Hunter, Beverly Luff, Beth Renner, Dorothy Tuttle, Leonard Walker, Frank Whitbeck, Danny Daniels, Matt Mattox, Bert May, Dorothy Raye, Victor Cox, Gary Gray, Victor Kilian, Robert Emmett O'Connor, Billy Royle, John Phipps, the Music Maids, and Group Seckler

The Early Years—*Meet Me in St. Louis* (1944)

Released November 22, 1944 (premiere)
MGM
113 minutes
Technicolor

Producer Arthur Freed was a sentimental man. So was Louis B. Mayer. As a result, when Freed got the idea to do a movie version of Sally Benson's book about her wholesome family in turn-of-the-century St. Louis, he believed he could convince Mayer to okay the project. It was Freed who came up with Judy Garland's line in *The Wizard of Oz*, "There's no place like home." He centered on that line in his concept for *Meet Me in St. Louis*.

Louis B. Mayer never read scripts. He had a couple of assistants who would tell him the stories and he would decide if they were worth filming. Arthur Freed enlisted the help of one of these women, Lillie Messinger, whose storytelling skills really connected with Mayer. She successfully presented Sally Benson's stories about a happy, financially comfortable family in St. Louis who are upset about the father's promotion because it means moving to New York. The MGM brass were not interested in what they thought was an old fashioned and mawkish idea. Mayer, however, connected with the sentiment, just as Freed thought he would.

Arthur Freed already planned to star Judy Garland in the movie, and thus hired one of her favorite screenwriters, Fred Finklehoffe, to write the screenplay. The usually confident Finkelhoffe believed this subject was too far out of his wheelhouse, so he asked, and received, permission to include Irving Brecher as his co-writer. The script, which was originally conceived as a small period picture, was completed in six weeks. After that, Finklehoffe, believing he had finished the project, departed for another job.

Freed decided to open up the picture and make a musical. So Brecher re-did the script from that concept after the producer received support from Mayer. The MGM brass continued to think that this was not a good idea, and were even more adamant when told the budget was going to be expanded for a musical. Mayer held firm, continuing to trust Freed's instincts. Vincente Minnelli was hired as the film's director and assisted Brecher with revamping the script. The two worked well together, and the result was a screenplay that effectively fit Freed's vision.

Judy Garland, however, didn't want to do the movie. She believed

The Films of Judy Garland

Poster for *Meet Me in St Louis*.

The Early Years—*Meet Me in St. Louis* (1944)

that while she'd be top billed, the real star of the narrative would be played by child actor Margaret O'Brien, a newcomer to MGM who made quite an impact with her first couple of movies. Brecher and Minnelli eventually convinced her that her part was the most important. Another conflict for Garland was that she didn't want to play another adolescent, especially being 21 and married and divorced. But the character of Esther was not the same as the teens she used to play, and Garland ultimately turns in a very sincere performance. It also helps that she was made to feel very beautiful in this movie for the first time, thanks both to Minnelli and makeup artist Dotty Ponedel, whom Garland would want to do her makeup from then on. Also, regardless of any supposed conflicts between the actresses playing the sisters, they all have fantastic chemistry and are really believable as a family.

Freed's vision became increasingly more opulent, and expensive. Originally to be shot on what was called the Andy Hardy street (because it depicted small town Americana), that was now not good enough. Freed hired Broadway designer Lemuel Ayers to join MGM art director Jack Martin Smith, and together they created a set that would respond to the Technicolor cinematography that the producer had decided upon. While all of this was going on, Freed continued to isolate himself from the MGM brass who thought this entire production was going to be a resounding flop that would negatively affect all of the careers associated with it.

Authenticity was important in recreating the period, and the art director knew it. As indicted in John Sturdevant's column in the *San Francisco Examiner*:

> There is no period in history as full of headaches for movie directors as that of the late 1890's and early 1900's. Get a ruffle out of place, or a curtain draped where it should have been "swagged" and hundreds of letters come pouring in to the studios from people "who were there." *Meet Me in St. Louis*, Metro Goldwyn Mayer's forthcoming Technicolor production, starring Judy Garland, is a case in point. A healthy percentage of the people who will see this screen drama remember those "good old days" vividly. Pictures set in periods a hundred or more years' ago offer no such problem. Research books on that era contradict one another and one person's guess is as good as another's. But when there are living witnesses to make-believe, it is a tough proposition to recreate it accurately enough to suit them.[50]

Opening in the summer of 1903, Judy Garland plays Esther Smith, one of five children of Alonzo Smith (Leon Ames), and his wife Anna

(Mary Astor). The other children are daughters Rose (Lucille Bremer), Agnes (Joan Carroll), and Tootie (Margaret O'Brien), and a son, Lon Jr. (Henry H. Daniels, Jr.). Esther is in love with next door neighbor John Truitt (Tom Drake). Rose hopes that her beau Warren Sheffield (Robert Sully) will propose to her. Rose discovers that Warren has a date for an upcoming dance, so she enlists her brother and some friends to purposely fill the dance card of Lucille Ballard (June Lockhart), but is surprised to find she is warm and friendly, not a pretentious Easterner like she figured. Agnes and Tootie get into mischief on Halloween when Tootie cries and concocts a wild story that John Truitt tried to kill her. Esther reacts angrily, running next door and hitting a confused John, until she finds that it was just a tall tale. All of these episodes come to a head when Alonzo announces to the family that he has been promoted and they'll be moving to New York after Christmas. The family is so firmly settled into their upper-middle-class existence in the quiet Midwest that the idea of moving to the big city is intimidating, especially regarding how it will disrupt their lives. Also, the World's Fair is about to open in St. Louis, a major event that they would all be missing. Alonzo, eventually realizing how much it would devastate his happy family, decides to stay in St. Louis.

Meet Me in St. Louis is a significant movie on many levels. It began the successful Arthur Freed–Vincente Minnelli collaborations. It began a veritable golden age of MGM musicals that would continue for twenty years. It produced some classic songs. It made a star of Margaret O'Brien. And, it not only introduced Garland to her second husband, it offered her a role that she played with both adult wisdom and youthful exuberance. Judy Garland was already a star, but with this film she became a more layered actress with a deeper and more complex and brilliant approach to her screen characters.

Cinematically, Vincente Minnelli proved himself to a be a brilliant director, with the movie's flow of movement and bright use of color enhancing the committed performances. The MGM brass was essentially correct. *Meet Me in St. Louis* really is a folksy, sentimental tale with episodes and vignettes tying together in the end, rather than a linear plot structure. What the brass didn't realize, and what both Freed and Mayer certainly knew, was that there was a large chunk of the nation that related completely to life in the Midwest. And since its turn-of-the-century setting offered nostalgia as well, it became embraced as a simpler, happier time by all moviegoers during a tension-filled period with a world war raging.

The Early Years—*Meet Me in St. Louis* (1944)

Judy Garland and Tom Drake in *Meet Me in St Louis*.

However, *Meet Me in St. Louis* was also fraught with problems. Along with the usual on-set injuries, there was a series of illnesses among cast members. Mary Astor had bouts with the flu, keeping her home. Harry Davenport was up in his 70s and also appearing in another film on the lot, so he succumbed to exhaustion and needed to take days off. Margaret O'Brien's mother felt her young daughter was working too hard, and called her in sick from January 31 until February 15, causing delays in production that became quite costly. Just after that, Joan Carroll had an appendicitis attack, needing surgery, which caused more delays. During Joan Carroll's absence, Judy Garland became ill, which laid off the entire company. Despite all of this, Vincente Minelli maintained a directorial pace and kept the company positive.

Meet Me in St. Louis is not a typical musical where songs pop up every few minutes. The music is carefully presented at proper intervals and, thus, has greater impact. The title song and the upbeat "Trolley Song" are particular highlights. But the biggest musical number is Judy Garland's soulful rendition of "Have Yourself a Merry Little Christmas," sung to Margaret O'Brien as the two look out her window at their St. Louis back yard for what they believe is the last time. Melodically beautiful and emotionally stirring, it is alongside "Over the Rainbow" as Garland's finest musical performance to date. She initially rejected the song. Its original lyrics were rather dark and unsettling. They were changed to being more optimistic, and this suited her, and the movie itself. Most of the main cast sang, but Leon Ames's singing was dubbed by Arthur Freed himself.

Perhaps *Meet Me in St. Louis* is more a movie with songs than a musical. Even the majority of the songs, like "Have Yourself a Merry Little Christmas" and "The Boy Next Door," are more intimate rather than the big splashy numbers found in most musicals. Because of the former song and the climax occurring on Christmas Eve, the film has become a holiday classic in addition to an all-around classic.

Vincente Minnelli was so particular about details that he worked very closely with original author Sally Benson in order to accurately present her home as she remembered it. He had some conflicts with Judy Garland not only due to her extending the production with delays and absences, but because he liked to rehearse and she did not. Garland would often try to flee the set after shooting her scenes to avoid subsequent rehearsals.

Because of its opulence and the various delays, *Meet Me in St. Louis* was an expensive production. However, despite the misgivings of the MGM brass, it grossed over four times its production costs, was hailed by both critics and moviegoers, and became the studio's highest grossing film since *Gone with the Wind* (1939). It was the second highest grossing movie in 1944, after *Going My Way*.

Meet Me in St. Louis earned four Academy Award nominations, including Best Writing (Adapted Screenplay), Best Color Cinematography, Best Music Scoring, and Best Song for "The Trolley Song." Margaret O'Brien received a special Academy Award for her work in this and other films that year. In 1994, *Meet Me in St. Louis* was deemed "culturally, historically, or aesthetically significant" by the Library of Congress and selected for preservation in the United States National Film Registry.

Meet Me in St. Louis was remade as a TV movie in 1959 with Jane Powell, Jeanne Crain, Patty Duke, Walter Pidgeon, Ed Wynn, Tab

The Early Years—*Meet Me in St. Louis* (1944)

Vincente Minnelli and Judy Garland didn't always get along on the set, but they married a year later.

Hunter, and Myrna Loy using the original Irving Brecher and Fred Finklehoffe screenplay. It was remade for television again in 1966 as a non-musical with Shelley Fabares, Celeste Holm, Larry Merrill, Judy Land, Reta Shaw, Tammy Locke, and Morgan Brittany, from a script written by original author Sally Benson. This proposed pilot for a TV series was not picked up.

Despite her initial misgivings, Judy Garland would later recall *Meet*

Judy Garland and Margaret O'Brien.

Me in St. Louis as among her finest films. She had just completed work on her next film, *The Clock*, when *Meet Me in St. Louis* premiered at Loew's State Theater in St. Louis on November 22, 1944, so she was not in attendance. However, Garland did attend the New York premiere two days later, and it was there that she announced her engagement to Vincente Minnelli.

The Early Years—*The Clock* (1945)

The Clock

Directed by Vincente Minnelli
Screenplay by Robert Nathan and Joseph Schrank (from a story by Paul and Pauline Gallico)
Produced by Arthur Freed
Cinematography by George J. Folsey
Film editing by George White
Cast: Judy Garland, Robert Walker, James Gleason, Keenan Wynn, Marshall Thompson, Lucile Gleason, Ruth Brady, Eddie Acuff, Sally Ann Brown, Wally Cassell, Chester Clute, Arthur Space, Robert Homan, Florence Allen, Jack Arkin, Jessie Arnold, Paulita Arvizu, King Baggot, Gertrude Hoffman, Milton Kibbee, Gary Gray, Teddy Infuhr, Joan Carroll, William Bailey, E.J. Ballantin, Charles Bates, Jack Baxley, Bunny Beatty, Barbara Bedford, Mary Benoit, Margaret Bert, Mary Bovard, Volta Boyer, Al Bridge, Steve Brodie, Ralph Brooks, Wheaton Chambers, Eddy Chandler, Paul E. Burns, Jack Carrington, Tony Carson, Douglas Carter, Lucille Casey, Dick Earle, George Dudley, Lyle Clark, Carol Coombs, Joe Dominguez, Lucille Curtis, Ruby Dandridge, Sarah Edwards, Dick Elliot, Arthur Freed, Charles Ferguson, Franklin Farnum, Kay English, Jane Green, Kenner Kemp, Sam Harris, Charlotte Knight, Herbert Gunn, Eddie Hall, Bobby Johnson, Jimmy Kelly, Patricia Knox, Robert Milasch, Michael Knudsen, Jack Lee, Sybil Merritt, Moyna Macgill, Babe London, Phil Morris, Jack Mower, Bill Phillips, Rudy Rama, Garry Owen, Robert Emmett O'Connor, Larry Steers, Doris Stone, Ray Teal, Nella Walker, Jean Wong, Ned Winchester, Ethel Tobin, Alice Wallace, Terry Moore, Thomas Murray, Alix Nagy, John Mylong, Peter Miles, and Richard Hall
Released May 25, 1945
MGM
90 minutes
Black and White

After spending some time requesting to be allowed to act in a non-musical drama, Judy Garland finally got that opportunity with *The Clock*, which was to be her only non-musical for MGM, as well as her last black and white movie until *Judgement at Nuremberg* sixteen years later. Musicals were Garland's strong suit, but they were also very grueling, and the studio had her making one after another. She'd still be performing in one film and already rehearsing for her next. Garland longed to do a movie set in current times, where she'd be wearing contemporary clothing and could act in a dramatic role without singing.

Arthur Freed with Judy Garland.

The Early Years—*The Clock* (1945)

Arthur Freed was building his reputation at MGM as a producer of musicals but he also wanted to explore producing a straight drama. He bought the movie rights to Paul and Pauline Gallico's short story "The Clock" and got MGM screenwriters active on a script for a film in which he planned to star Judy Garland, with Robert Walker as the male lead.

For a director, Freed hired Fred Zinnemann, who had spent the 1930s directing short films and broke into feature films with *Kid Glove Killer* (1942). While only a B-level second-feature, *Kid Glove Killer* was brought in on a budget and earned a nice profit. However, an attempt to start a B-level series about blind detective Duncan "Mac" Maclain with the film *Eyes of the Night* (1942) was not a success. But, Zinnemann proved himself to the MGM brass when he helmed an A-movie for the studio, *The Seventh Cross* (1944), starring Spencer Tracy, and it was a success. Freed felt Zinnemann would be a good director for *The Clock*.

Judy Garland, however, had other ideas. While she had nothing against Zinnemann, she wanted her new fiancée Vincente Minnelli to direct the film. Meanwhile, Zinnemann realized the project wasn't quite for him after working on it for a few weeks. Garland's approach didn't mesh with Zinnemann's at all. He spoke with Freed, who had already heard from Garland, and was amicably removed from the project. Vincente Minnelli was hired. Interestingly enough, *The Clock* was a drama about having to get as much done as possible in a limited amount of time, and that would be similar in concept to what would be the basic premise of Fred Zinnemann's directorial masterpiece, *High Noon* (1952).

Vincente Minnelli saw what Zinnemann had shot and was dissatisfied, so he scrapped all of the footage and started from the beginning. Just as he had with *Meet Me in St. Louis*, Minnelli directed *The Clock* with very careful and precise attention to detail. Filming on location was difficult and expensive during this time, so Minnelli effectively recreated contemporary New York City on the MGM lot, even arranging a reconstruction of Penn Station at a cost of $66,450. He also changed aspects of the script, which annoyed screenwriter Bob Nathan, who took the issue to Arthur Freed. Minnelli defended his decision, stating, "There was a scene with a little boy at the pond in Central Park. Bob Walker made friends with him in the original script. It was all terribly 'darling.' Instead, I made him kick Walker and that made him more real, more human."[51] The result was a visually stunning film that was filled with remarkable directorial touches as well as strong, gripping performances by both Robert Walker and Judy Garland.

Judy Garland plays Alice Mayberry, who is hurrying to a crowded subway station when she trips over a soldier's foot as he sits out front. The soldier is Joe Allen (Robert Walker), a small-town boy who is making a two-day stop in New York City before going into combat with his unit. Joe feels badly that he is indirectly responsible for Alice breaking her heel, and takes her to a shoe shop to get it repaired. Longing

Judy Garland breaks her heel and Robert Walker helps her in *The Clock*.

The Early Years—*The Clock* (1945)

for a friend during his short time in New York, the aimless Joe hangs around with Alice, who is suspicious at first but eventually realizes this homespun serviceman is genuine and harmless. After spending a fun day visiting the Central Park Zoo and the Metropolitan Museum of Art, Alice has to leave, but they arrange to meet under the clock at the Astor Hotel. When Alice reveals all of this to her skeptical roommate, she is chided for trusting Joe, who is basically a stranger. The two meet late, have dinner, but miss the last bus home, so they ride with a milkman (James Gleason) and later spend a nice morning with him and his wife (Lucile Gleason, the actor's real-life wife). Joe and Alice are separated in a crowded subway and realize neither knows the other's last name. They each, separately, get the idea to go back to the subway station where they first met, and are reunited. Realizing by the brief separation that they are in love, they hastily rush through a marriage. Although it is legal, Alice cries over how rushed and impersonal it was, so they go into a church and quietly repeat their vows for each other while sitting in a pew. By this time, Joe's two-day leave has ended and he must return to the battlefield.

In its first moments, *The Clock* is immediately impressive due to Vincente Minnelli's directorial vision. Joe leaves the train into New York City, and his small-town sensibilities are shocked by the crowded train station. Minnelli conveys this by presenting constant movement within the frame, filling the negative space surrounding Joe with people hustling to their next destination. Even when Joe stops to ask how to get out of subway station and into the street, the man he stops to ask is polite in his response, but obviously in quite a rush. Minnelli brilliantly conveys how quickly life moves in the big city, further emphasizing Joe's limited time frame and how much can be done in 48 hours. Alice is not a New York native, but came to the city three years earlier, and has comfortably settled into its rhythm with a job, her own place, and a general distrust of strangers, but not so deeply that she has forgotten how to recognize the basic goodness of a small-town tourist.

Both of the actors are somewhere near their best. Robert Walker had been playing comical parts until a great dramatic turn in *Since You Went Away* (1943)—a drama about the home front during World War II—showed the depth of his talent. Fresh faced and brimming with boyish innocence, Walker masterfully conveys through his nuanced performance an alternately intimidated and fascinated reaction to New York City, and his initial attraction growing into deep infatuation for Garland's character. Though devoid of the glamour exhibited in some previous

The Films of Judy Garland

pictures, Judy Garland is at her most naturally beautiful in *The Clock*. She is an ordinary working girl in the big city who is both focused and driven, and not quite ready for the distraction of a lonely soldier on a weekend pass. But Joe offers Alice the type of man she no longer sees in the big city—one that reminds her of the comfort, safety, and innocence of small-town life. At first her attraction is due to sentiment, but she responds more strongly when she realizes the affection he feels for her.

Everything works in *The Clock*, from the director's continued fast pace on the margins of the frame, to the nuanced performances of both actors. The happy highs and sad lows alternate with a perfect rhythm. The background music rises slowly and reaches crescendo at just the right times. The story allows the characters to develop as the central part of the narrative.

It is worth noting how both time and the city of New York serve as major supporting characters in this movie. The viewer is almost always cognizant of the clock ticking down and the time for Alice and Joe to be together running out, especially in the scenes where they are rushing to jump through all the hoops required to get married before the office closes. The movie is romantic, but doesn't sugarcoat anything. The idea of getting married on a whim is very romantic but not super practical, as the movie shows. The comparison-contrast between their drab civil ceremony and the exchanging of vows in the church is very revealing. Joe and especially Alice realize the magnitude of what they have done (their dinner together afterwards is sort of awkward, like now they don't really know what to say to each other). But the brief scene in a hotel room the morning after their wedding and Alice's reaction to Joe's leaving (she walks away smiling, not sad or crying), suggests a hopeful future for the couple. Of course, there's a lot still up in the air—there's always the chance that Joe won't come home from the war.

According to Hugh Fordin in his book about Arthur Freed's productions, *World of Entertainment: Hollywood's Greatest Musicals*:

> *The Clock* was Freed's first dramatic picture. To cast Judy Garland in the role of a plain, lower middle-class girl, in a milieu of drabness, took a man of Freed's convictions. He entrusted Minnelli with the direction although he had exclusively worked in the medium of musical comedy, both on stage and screen. Freed's daring antitype casting brought to the screen an exceptionally sensitive, touching film that one could describe as the love story of that era.[52]

Critics were pleased with Judy Garland's appearance in a straight non-musical drama and were positive when reviewing the film. The *New*

The Early Years—*The Clock* (1945)

Judy Garland and Robert Walker fall in love in *The Clock*.

York Times stated: "A tender and refreshingly simple romantic drama. The atmosphere of the big town has seldom been conveyed more realistically upon the screen; the kind of picture that leaves one with a warm feeling toward his fellow man, especially towards the young folks who today are trying to crowd a lifetime of happiness into a few fleeting hours." The *New York Daily News* stated, "The sweetest, most tender drama yet produced about a soldier and a girl. Judy Garland and Robert Walker are perfectly cast as the modest, sincere girl and the shy, sincere boy."[53]

The only problem *The Clock* had was its own timing. By the time it was released in 1945, the war was wrapping up, it was obvious the Allies would win, and a war-weary moviegoing public wanted the escape of musical comedy, not a drama about a soldier's brief romance while headed back to the battlefield. If released even a year earlier, *The Clock* would have been an enormous success. However, while it did make a profit, by comparison to something like *Meet Me in St. Louis*, the profit was marginal.

Judy Garland followed this by doing another guest shot in an all-star MGM musical entitled *Ziegfeld Follies*. It is notable as having Fred Astaire and Gene Kelly dance together, and to feature Red Skelton's hilarious "Guzzler's Gin" routine, among other vignettes. Garland's segment was originally supposed to feature Greer Garson, but she eventually decided it wasn't for her. Vincente Minnelli was directing the film (replacing George Sidney, who left the project), so he arranged for Judy Garland to replace Greer Garson. Garland also attended the Boston premiere with Vincente Minnelli.

Despite showing her talent for drama in *The Clock*, it was obvious the public wanted escapist fare after the war, and especially wanted Judy Garland in musicals. It would be another sixteen years before she played in a dramatic film without singing.

Arrangements were made for Garland to follow *The Clock* by starring opposite Fred Astaire in Vincente Minnelli's next assigned directorial effort, *Yolanda and the Thief*. This delighted Garland, because she wanted to work with Fred Astaire. Unfortunately, the studio changed its collective mind. A dramatic feature with a western setting that was to star Lana Turner was revamped into a western musical after MGM noticed the success of *Oklahoma* performed on stage. Garland was taken off the Minnelli-Astaire project and placed into *The Harvey Girls*.

The Harvey Girls

Directed by George Sidney
Screenplay by Edmund Beloin, Nathaniel Curtis, Harry Crane,
    James O'Hanlon, Samson Raphaelson, and Kay Van Riper (from
    an original story by Eleanore Griffin and William Rankin, based
    on the novel by Samuel Hopkins Adams)
Produced by Arthur Freed
Cinematography by George J. Folsey
Film editing by Albert Akst
Songs:
    The music for all of the songs was composed by Harry Warren,
        and Johnny Mercer wrote all of the lyrics.
    "On the Atchison, Topeka, and the Santa Fe"
    "In the Valley (Where the Evenin' Sun Goes Down)"

The Early Years—*The Harvey Girls* (1946)

"Wait and See"
"The Train Must Be Fed"
"Oh, You Kid"
"It's a Great Big World"
"The Wild, Wild West"
"Swing Your Partner Round and Round"
Cast: Judy Garland, John Hodiak, Ray Bolger, Angela Lansbury, Preston Foster, Virginia O'Brien, Kenny Baker, Marjorie Main, Chill Wills, Selena Ryle, Cyd Charisse, Ruth Brade, Jack Lambert, Edward Earle, Morris Ankrum, Bill Phillips, Ben Carter, Norman Leavett, Stephen McNally, William Hall, Virginia Hunter, Catherine McLeod, Byron Harvey, Jr., Michell Lewis, Vernon Dent, Robert Emmett O'Connor, Jane Allen, Jean Ashton, Eleanor Bayley, Joan Carey, Lucille Casey, Ruth Clark, Virginia Davis, Meredyth Durrell, Mary Jo Ellis, Mary Jane French, Virginia Gumm, Gloria Hope, Janet Lavis, Loulie Jean Norman, Shirley Patterson, Joan Thorsen, Dorothy Tuttle, Dorothy Wilkerson, Katherine Yorke, Dallas Worth, Herberta Williams, Eve Whitney, Bunny Waters, Tyra Vaughn, Dorothy Van Nuys, Elinor Troy, Melba Snowden, Nevada Smith, Erin Selwyn, Edith Motridge, Peggy Maley, Emily Smith, Maxine Leslie, Verna Lee, Thelma Joel, Jane Hall, Kay English, Virginia Donovan, Dona Dax, Georgia Davis, Jane Hale, Hazel Brooks, Frank Austin, John Barton, Phil Bloom, Chet Brandenburg, Rand Brooks, Ewing Miles Brown, Jack Rube Clifford, Tex Cooper, Victor Cox, Vivian Edwards, Sam Garrett, Vincent Graeff, Stuart Hall, George Huggins, Dorothy Jackson, Joe Karnes, Jack Kenny, Al Kunde, Johnny Luther, Claude Martin, Judy Matson, Matt Mattox, John Merton, Mary Moder, Paul Newlan, Jack Perry, Lee Phelps, Tom Quinn, Charles Regan, Al Rhein, John Rice, Kenneth Rundquist, Harry Semels, Ray Teal, Al Thompson, Jim Toney, and Marica Van Dyke
Released January 18, 1946 (Hollywood Premiere)
MGM
102 minutes
Technicolor

Back in a Technicolor musical after her outstanding dramatic performance in *The Clock,* Judy Garland was really not supposed to be in this movie at all. It was not supposed to be a Technicolor musical. As indicated in the previous chapter, *The Harvey Girls* was originally going to be a straight story featuring Lana Turner. The rights to the book had been purchased for that project in 1942. But, just like *Presenting*

The Films of Judy Garland

Lily Mars, the concept was changed to a musical production. The success of *Oklahoma* on Broadway gave producer Arthur Freed the idea to make a western-based musical of his own.

The movie was based on a book about an actual chain of restaurants owned by Fred Harvey. The Harvey Company was unhappy with the book and was skeptical about MGM making it into a movie. Freed's assistant producer, Roger Edens, went to the Harvey headquarters in Chicago, Illinois, and presented the MGM idea for a musical. The company approved, but only under the condition that its late founder, Fred Harvey, not be portrayed in the film, and that the movie was wholesome and family oriented. These were accepted by the studio. At least one actual Harvey relative, Byron Harvey, Jr., does have a cameo in the film, doing a brief scene with veteran comedy actor Vernon Dent.

Judy Garland returned to musicals after her non-singing drama.

Judy Garland plays Susan Bradley, who is traveling by train to Sandrock, Arizona, to meet a man with whom she connected through a Lonelyhearts ad. After exchanging several beautiful, romantic letters, they plan to meet and marry. While traveling, Susan meets several women who are new waitresses for the Harvey House restaurants. Upon arrival, Susan finds that her correspondent is an old man (Chill Wills) who didn't write the letters at all, but actually had his eloquent friend, saloon owner Ned Trent (John Hodiak), write them. Susan and the old man reach a mutual understanding and call off their "engagement," such as it is, but she remains highly offended by Trent's hand in this and lets him know. Her fiery scolding attracts Trent. This upsets saloon singer Em (Angela Lansbury), who is in love with Trent. Susan joins up with

The Early Years—*The Harvey Girls* (1946)

the Harvey Girls while Trent has Judge Sam Purvis (Preston Foster) try to scare them off, believing the restaurant to be competition for his saloon. Eventually, Trent realizes the worthiness of the chain restaurant and tells Purvis to back off, but he refuses, burning down the restaurant. Trent offers his own saloon as a replacement, so Em and the dance hall girls leave town. Susan does also, believing Trent himself is leaving since he gave up his saloon. On the train, rival Em has a heart-to-heart talk with Susan and the train stops as she sees Trent hurriedly riding his horse after the train for her.

While the romance between Susan and Ned is a big part of the film, from the start the film sets up the main conflict as being between the untamed West and progress, between "bad girls" and "good girls" (the saloon girls and the Harvey girls even literally fight toward the end of the film). There's a lot of contrast both in the behaviors of the types of characters Lansbury and Garland play, but also in their costumes (the sparkling, sultry gowns Em wears versus the staid uniform of the Harvey girls). It's also interesting that, despite the nice final scene between Em and Susan on the train, there isn't really a reconciliation that redeems the saloon girls or that forces them to change their ways. Rather than coexisting with the Harvey girls and the progress they represent, they leave town. Even as she is leaving the saloon for the last time, Em looks disdainfully at the previously nude statues on the stairs that are now wearing modest dresses.

This is also a really

Judy Garland appeared as a Harvey Girl waitress in *The Harvey Girls*.

The Films of Judy Garland

Judy Garland and John Hodiak in *The Harvey Girls*.

great role for Judy Garland, allowing her to utilize all her talents: dramatic acting, singing and dancing, and comedy. She's really funny in this movie and has a good amount of physical comedy, especially in the sequence where she grabs a pair of six shooters she doesn't know how to use, in an attempt to steal back the Harvey restaurant steaks from the saloon.

One of the most significant aspects of *The Harvey Girls* is the song "On the Atchinson, Topeka, and the Santa Fe," which was not only a highlight in the film but was used to help promote it. MGM had the song recorded and released as a record while the movie was still in production. It was a big hit, with recordings by Bing Crosby, The Merry Macs, Tommy Dorsey, and, of course, Judy Garland. The song entered the Billboard charts in July 1945 and remained there throughout the summer and fall, with several

The Early Years—*The Harvey Girls* (1946)

versions enjoying strong chart status. A version by Johnny Mercer, for instance, stayed at number one for sixteen weeks. Bing Crosby's recording got as far as number four on the charts. Garland's hit number one on Your Hit Parade for eight weeks. In the movie, she performed "On the Atchison, Topeka, and the Santa Fe" in one take, showing her continued professionalism.

Ann Sothern was originally to be cast as Em, but she gave birth to her child (actress Tisha Sterling) on December 10, 1944, just as filming was about to commence (Judy Garland first reported to the set on December 29). Sothern was replaced by Angela Lansbury, a relative newcomer to films, but who also had already been nominated for an Oscar (for *Gaslight*). Curiously, although Lansbury was a trained vocalist, her singing was dubbed in *The Harvey Girls* (she would later win Tony Awards for her singing performances in the musicals *Mame* and *Sweeney Todd*).

Ann Sothern's wasn't the only pregnancy that potentially disrupted the production. Supporting player Virginia O'Brien, becoming known as "the deadpan singer" due to her lack of expression when she sang, was

Angela Lansbury and Judy Garland play rivals in *The Harvey Girls*.

pregnant during production and started to show before filming concluded. Thus, she is not seen a lot during the second half of the movie.

Regarding the other supporting players, Cyd Charisse was making her debut in a role with dialogue, having previously appeared only as a dancer in a handful of films, including two in which Judy Garland also appeared (*Thousands Cheer* and *The Ziegfeld Follies*). Ray Bolger, so delightful as the Scarecrow in *The Wizard of Oz*, appears for the second, and final, time in a movie with Judy Garland. And, along with leading man John Hodiak, several actors from western movies were added for authenticity, including Preston Foster, Chill Wills, and Jack Lambert.

The Harvey Girls was an expensive production. The Freed unit received the support of MGM to spend the money necessary for the film to look opulent and colorful. This included $132,962 for the writers, $443,766.67 for the cast, and $75,942.38 for the costumes. The cost of the Sandrock Street set with exteriors and interiors for both the Alhambra and the Harvey House was $395,969.40. However, despite these expenses, *The Harvey Girls* was another big box office hit, with moviegoers happy to see Judy Garland in a big colorful musical.

The initial preview was held in Inglewood, California, on July 12, 1945, after which the musical numbers "March of the Doagies" and "My Intuition" were cut from the production. Both musical numbers were filmed, and the footage has survived, appearing as extras on some DVD versions of the movie. Another song, "Hayride," was prerecorded but wasn't filmed. *The Harvey Girls* premiered on January 18, 1946, at the Capitol Theater in New York City, and thereafter went into wide release. One of the more creative promotional ideas happened at the first Midwest showing of *The Harvey Girls* when twin premieres were held at the Orpheum Theater in Atchison, Kansas, and the Grand Theater in Topeka, Kansas. The song "On the Atchison, Topeka, and the Santa Fe" was the tie-in, when the Santa Fe shipped a miniature streamlined train to the Atchison as the feature attraction of a parade immediately preceding the premiere. The costume worn by Judy Garland was shipped to Atchison from Hollywood, and the theater presented a special window display.

Critics were impressed with *The Harvey Girls*. *Film Daily* commented on how expensive the production was: "Produced without pinching by Arthur Freed, *The Harvey Girls*, dressed up in Technicolor adding to the film's sense of excitement, is an expensive and vivid show full of spirit and exuberance."[54] Bosley Crowther at the *New York Times* stated, with typical stodginess, "Miss Garland, of course, is at the center of most of the activity and handles herself in pleasing fashion, up to and

The Early Years—*The Pirate* (1948)

including the high notes. John Hodiak acts rather surly as the saloon proprietor and Angela Lansbury, pouty and pomaded, looks dazzling as the queen of the den. Everyone else enters lightly into this beefsteak and hors d'oeuvre opera. It may be a rather lofty tribute to Fred Harvey's girls, but it's a show."[55]

Despite the expenses, *The Harvey Girls* grossed nearly twice its production costs. The hit song highlight, "On the Atchison, Topeka, and the Santa Fe," won the Academy Award for Best Original Song.

After she finished *The Harvey Girls*, Judy Garland married Vincente Minnelli on June 15, 1945, and went on a ten-week honeymoon. Upon their return in September, Garland was among a number of celebrity cameos seen in the all-star MGM musical *Till the Clouds Roll By*, directed by Richard Whorf. This was a highly fictional account of the life and career of songwriter Jerome Kern, played by Garland's co-star in *The Clock*, Robert Walker. Garland played singer-actress Marilyn Miller, and her new husband Vincente Minnelli directed her scenes. She was in the early stages of pregnancy with daughter Liza Minnelli when shooting her guest appearance in *Till the Clouds Roll By*.

With her starring role in the hit *The Harvey Girls*, and her guest shot in *Till the Clouds Roll By*, Judy Garland was at the top of her game and the height of her stardom. She had been a major MGM star for a couple of years at this point and was now at her peak. Unfortunately, things also started becoming much more difficult around this time. Preoccupied with her personal life, especially with her first child, and a marriage that started off blissfully but became increasingly more challenging, Judy Garland did not appear in another film for two years. While the press claimed Garland was taking some time off "to be a mother," that was only part of it. Raising the child might have been a central reason, but there were actually other pressures that made it necessary that she not immediately become active in another movie project.

The Pirate

Directed by Vincente Minnelli
Screenplay by Albert Hackett and Frances Goodrich (from the play by S.N. Behrman)

The Films of Judy Garland

Produced by Arthur Freed
Cinematography by Harry Stradling
Film editing by Blanche Sewell
Songs:
    All songs were composed by Cole Porter.
    "Nina"
    "Mack the Black"
    "You Can Do No Wrong"
    "Be a Clown"
    "Love of My Life"
Cast: Judy Garland, Gene Kelly, Walter Slezak, Gladys Cooper, Reginald Owen, George Zucco, Fayard and Harold Nicholas, Lester Allen, Lola Deem, Ellen Ross, Mary Jo Ellis, Jean Dean, Marion Murray, Ben Lessy, Jerry Bergen, Val Seitz, Cully Richards, Lola Albright, George Chandler, Oliver Blake, Dick Simmons, Anne Francis, Alex Romero, Fred Gilman, Marie Windsor, O.Z. Whitehead, Irene Vernon, Hamil Petroff, Dee Turnell, Marie Allison, Anne Beck, Suzette Harbin, Hal Bell, George Emerson, Norman Borine, Wheaton Chambers, Willa Pear Curtis, Jack Regas, Aurora Navarro, Jill Meredith, Jane Howard, Paul Maxey, Bert May, Sharon Saunders, and Dorothy Tuttle
MGM
Released June 11, 1948
102 minutes
Technicolor

As far as the public was concerned, Judy Garland was taking time off to raise her first child, daughter Liza, who was born March 12, 1946. Garland was off screen for all of 1947. It was the first year since 1936 that a new Judy Garland movie was not playing in theaters. However, during her time off, MGM made sure that Garland's name was still active in the press, with a number of announced projects.

As early as January 1947, Hedda Hopper's syndicated column claimed that Garland was to star in a remake of Jane Austen's *Pride and Prejudice*, already filmed by MGM in 1940. Hopper's column stated:

> Judy Garland tells me she plans spending a year in England, with, of course, her husband Vincente Minnelli and baby Liza. That doesn't mean she'll be off the screen that long. The chief purpose of the trip is to remake *Pride and Prejudice* in its original setting. Judy will star in it and Minnelli will direct. When Metro made this picture the last time, Greer Garson and Laurence Olivier were its stars. The story, adapted from the famous English classic, is being

The Early Years—*The Pirate* (1948)

revamped to include a number of songs for Garland although she insists it won't be a musical. Not that she objects to musicals. She loves them. But she likes to mix them with straight dramas, such as *The Clock*.[56]

Of course, this project never happened, nor did several other announcements that popped up during Judy's hiatus from movies. Such titles as *Years Ago* to co-star Garland and Spencer Tracy, and to be directed by Garson Kanin, and *Peg O' My Heart* with Robert Stack were among the movies she never did, and might have been just publicity from the studio to keep her name active in the press.

In 1945 and 1946, things seemed to be going exceptionally well for Judy Garland. She was satisfied with how she looked in a magazine cover photo (despite her usual insecurity about her looks), and was pleased with the variety and challenge of her most recent screen work (especially having done the non-musical drama *The Clock*). But by 1947, Garland was suffering from postpartum depression, and her psychological issues were shaken by some events. In February, she was named Worst Dressed Celebrity in a widely syndicated column that ignited her

Vincente Minnelli and Judy Garland flank baby Liza.

The Films of Judy Garland

insecurities. Her marriage to Vincente Minnelli was another factor, as he was often quite demanding despite her frailty. And yet, MGM still believed in Judy Garland and offered her a contract renewal where she'd be getting a then-significant $6000 per week and only be expected to make two films per year.

By the time Judy Garland returned to the screen, it was opposite Gene Kelly for the first time since his screen debut, *For Me and My Gal*. Kelly's star had risen quickly. His dancing in the Columbia feature *Cover Girl* with Rita Hayworth and Phil Silvers attracted moviegoers initially. Then his performance in the MGM musical *Anchors Aweigh* with newcomer Frank Sinatra not only allowed him to assist in the choreography, but included his iconic dance with Jerry the cartoon mouse. Gene Kelly's performance in *Anchors Aweigh* earned an Oscar nomination.

Kelly's stardom allowed him a large co-starring role in *The Pirate* opposite Judy Garland. Kelly continued to credit Garland for suggesting him for the role in *For Me and My Gal* and giving him this successful movie career. Thus, he was patient and supportive as she suffered mental breakdowns throughout the filming of *The Pirate*. The production was scheduled for 130 days. Garland missed 99 of them.

The Pirate was originally supposed to begin shooting in early December 1946. However, Garland was in no shape to work, even

Gene Kelly and Judy Garland in *The Pirate*.

The Early Years—*The Pirate* (1948)

though she showed up on the set. She had lost a great deal of weight, and her amphetamine usage was out of control. At one point, when producer Arthur Freed was walking by, Vincente Minnelli fell onto Garland as if he had stumbled and held her because she was reacting poorly to the drugs. According to Gerold Frank's biography:

> To add to Judy's problems, she was surrounded by sycophants. She believed very few people. She needed, yet found it difficult to endure, such excessive flattery. Nobody spoke to Judy about herself in anything but superlatives, particularly about her performances on the screen, and this was almost unbearable to her if it was not the truth.[57]

Garland was not able to return to the set and begin actual shooting until almost a month after she was originally scheduled. The film was completed in July 1947.

The Pirate features Judy Garland as Manuela Alva, a lonely girl who lives in Calvados, a small Caribbean village. She longs for adventure and dreams of being taken away by the legendary pirate Mack "the black" Macoco. However, the aunt and uncle who raised her have arranged that she marry the town mayor, Don Pedro (Walter Slezak). While visiting nearby Port Sebastian just before her wedding, she meets Serafin (Gene Kelly), a handsome, womanizing leader of a traveling circus. He falls for Manuela and hypnotizes her, hoping she'll proclaim her love for him, but she instead professes to love Macoco. Don Pedro arrives for his wedding to Manuela and Serafin recognizes him as Macoco, but he is now old and overweight. Don Pedro begs Serafin to not reveal his identity, lest he be hanged, so Serafin blackmails him into letting the circus perform there, and also takes on the identity of Macoco in order to entice Manuela to fall in love with him. Manuela eventually discovers the ruse and is angry, but has fallen in love with Serafin by this time. Don Pedro, meanwhile, tries to convince the law that Serafin is indeed Macoco and he should hang. Manuela eventually discovers that Don Pedro is indeed the real Macoco. He tries to capture Manuela but is attacked by Serafin's circus troupe.

The Pirate is really a costume adventure with music, not the typical musical with several songs. However, the Cole Porter numbers are delightful, especially "Be a Clown," which is one of the film's highlights. And despite Judy Garland's issues making the production a very difficult shoot, her performance is quite good and the movie itself is a delightful romantic adventure.

However, *The Pirate* is also a very daring production in that it is quite different than the typical musical adventure. Both Garland and Kelly perform with noisy dramatic flair, their intentional overacting calling attention to the off-kilter approach to the material. It is a lot of crazy fun for the right frame of mind, but some just find it forced and unappealing. Along with Garland and Kelly, Walter Slezak comfortably gets caught up in the proceedings and plays along with the comedy by exhibiting the same gusto as the film's stars.

The screenplay for *The Pirate* went through several rewrites before Frances Goodrich and Albert Hackett did the final rewrite. The songs were staged by Cole Porter himself, while Garland, who usually worked well with the songwriter, challenged him on some of the most trivial details. Some believe it was due to Garland being overmedicated.

Gene Kelly worked closely with choreographer Robert Alton, including coming up with dances that combined classical and popular styles, and realizing how camera angles made a difference in how the dances were shot. Kelly fought to get the team of Fayard and Harold Nicholas in the movie, but, sadly, in the segregated South, the first "Be a Clown" number, which featured them and Kelly, was sometimes cut. Only the song's reprise with Kelly and Garland was included.

Because of all the delays and problems, the budget for *The Pirate* soared to nearly $4 million. It only made back a bit over half that amount, resulting in *The Pirate* being the first Judy Garland movie to lose money at the box office since *The Wizard of Oz*. Critics were generally pleased; the *Los Angeles Times* stated:

> *The Pirate* is as gay and charming entertainment as anyone would care to see. MGM has produced a picture starring Judy Garland and Gene Kelly which is spontaneous, beautiful and intriguing to the very last moment. That moment, in fact, "Be a Clown," closing song, with comedy trimming, is practically, like the beginning of a new show and will make audiences feel as if they want to see the picture go right on. It is as clever a finale as revealed in any musical film in a long time.[58]

It can be argued that *The Pirate* has unfairly gotten a bad reputation over the years, because it was ahead of its time. Perhaps it didn't register at the time with some moviegoers that the film was a send-up of classic swashbucklers, and that it was set in a fantasy world, not meant to be a reflection of reality. Garland's previous musicals are all set firmly in the real world, with the musical numbers serving as occasional departures from reality before returning to it. It's very obvious that *The Pirate* was filmed on a soundstage inside (actually, the sets make it feel rather confined at times, which shouldn't be surprising since it's based on a play).

The Early Years—*Easter Parade* (1948)

The sets and costumes are absurdly bright and colorful. It's a really offbeat looking and sounding movie, but it's obvious that it was made to be intentionally campy, and on that level it works.

Judy Garland and Gene Kelly were next slated to co-star in the movie *Easter Parade*. Because of the difficulties between Garland and Vincente Minnelli, the director was to be Charles Walters, who had worked with her as a choreographer and was just starting to direct films. When Gene Kelly sprained his ankle and could not be in the movie, the studio summoned Fred Astaire, with whom Garland always wanted to work.

Easter Parade

Directed by Charles Walters
Screenplay by Sidney Sheldon, Albert Hackett, and Frances Goodrich (based on an original story by Hackett and Goodrich)
Produced by Arthur Freed
Cinematography by Harry Stradling
Film editing by Albert Akst
Songs:
    All songs were written by Irving Berlin.
    "Happy Easter"
    "Drum Crazy"
    "It Only Happens When I Dance with You"
    "Everybody's Doin' It"
    "I Want to Go Back to Michigan"
    "Beautiful Faces Need Beautiful Clothes"
    "A Fella with an Umbrella"
    "I Love a Piano"
    "Snooky Ookums"
    "Ragtime Violin"
    "When the Midnight Choo Choo Leaves for Alabam'"
    "Shakin' the Blues Away"
    "Steppin' Out with My Baby"
    "A Couple of Swells"
    "The Girl on the Magazine Cover"
    "Better Luck Next Time"
    "Easter Parade"

The Films of Judy Garland

Cast: Judy Garland, Fred Astaire, Ann Miller, Peter Lawford, Jules Munshin, Richard Beavers, Peter Chong, Doris Kemper, Jeni Le Gon, Dick Simmons, Joi Lansing, Wilson Wood, Ralph Sanford, Angi Poulos, Jean Romor, Laura Mason, Max Linder, Richard Neill, Robert Emmett O'Connor, Bert May, Lola Albright, Jimmie Dodd, Don Anderson, Bob Jellison, Patricia Edwards, JC Fowler, Patricia Jackson, Harry Fox, Marjorie Jackson, Joel Friend, Sig Frohlich, Shep Houghton, Helene Heigh, June Gale, John Albright, Jack Deery, James Conaty, Shirley Ballard, Jimmy Bates, Hal Bell, Gail Langford, King Lockwood, Nolan Leary, Dick Paxton, Sara Shane, Johnny Walsh, Benay Venuta, Harry Tenbrook, Dee Turnell, Bert Spencer, Bobbie Priest, and Lulu Mae Bohrman
MGM
Released July 8, 1948
103 minutes
Technicolor

Judy Garland's longing to work with Fred Astaire was fulfilled with *Easter Parade*, even though it didn't start out that way. However, the film ended up co-starring Garland and Astaire and was among the best films in either performer's entire screen career.

Easter Parade came about from the mind of songwriter Irving Berlin, who had the concept and took it to 20th Century Fox. Berlin had enjoyed success with *Alexander's Ragtime Band* (1938) with Fox, so he presented the idea for a film using some popular songs from his existing catalog, along with new ones he'd compose for the film. Fox didn't like Berlin's terms, which included $600,000 in pay and a percentage of the subsequent film's profits. He then approached MGM producer Arthur Freed. While MGM agreed to the $600,000 fee, there would be no percentage. It didn't matter. Irving Berlin was eager to have Judy Garland sing his songs.

Easter Parade is not only one of Judy Garland's best and most successful musicals, it was also one of her happiest experiences making a movie—a real departure from the tumult of filming *The Pirate*. However, this wasn't the case at the outset. Originally, Vincente Minnelli was set to direct the film, but Garland's psychiatrist believed that after *The Pirate,* the two should not work together again so quickly. Shortly after *The Pirate* wrapped in July 1947, Garland attempted suicide. She was placed in a sanitarium until August, and by September she was in rehearsals for *Easter Parade.* According to Gerold Frank's biography:

The Early Years—*Easter Parade* (1948)

Fred Astaire and Judy Garland teamed up in *Easter Parade*.

Vincente was crushed. In a kind of desperation, to help him cope with what was going on both at the studio and at home, he sought out an analyst himself, and after a few weeks, Vincente, who had been under intense pressure, was able to accept this new state of affairs and begin to busy himself with other work. He and Judy did not even talk about his removal.[59]

The director job was given to Charles Walters, who was a dance director that Garland had always liked. He had just recently moved behind the camera. Meanwhile, Irving Berlin got the rights to work on the eight contracted new songs for the movie. According to Hugh Fordin's book on Freed's musicals:

> With great zest, Berlin threw himself into writing new songs for what he termed "the younger generation," Judy Garland and Gene Kelly. They included "Better Luck Next Time," "A Fella with an Umbrella," "It Only Happens When I Dance with You," "Drum Crazy," "Steppin' Out with My Baby," and "Happy Easter." But Freed also felt the picture needed a fun number for the two stars. Berlin agreed to write it, even though he had completed the eight new songs as per his contract. He returned with "Let's Take an Old-Fashioned Walk,"

The Films of Judy Garland

which Freed didn't care for. Berlin replied, "You don't like it? Forget about it—I'll use it somewhere else." An hour later, Berlin had written "A Couple of Swells." Freed loved it.[60]

When Charles Walters took the job, he read the script by Albert Hackett and Frances Goodrich and was horrified. Inspired, perhaps, by Gene Kelly's popular performance in *Pal Joey* on Broadway, they made his character a ruthless, abusive musical star who maintained his popularity by being negatively aggressive toward others. Garland's character would take the brunt of the abuse. Walters met with Gene Kelly and Judy Garland and explained that the audiences would hate the character

Irving Berlin was delighted to write for old friend Fred Astaire and a happy Judy Garland.

The Early Years—*Easter Parade* (1948)

Kelly played and he would not be able to redeem it in the end, especially since Garland was so beloved by audiences. Besides the fact, Kelly had garnered a pretty strong following of his own, and they responded to his affable, good-guy persona. Screenwriter Sidney Sheldon won a Best Screenplay Oscar for his pleasant, light comedy *The Bachelor and the Bobby-Soxer*—an RKO release starring Cary Grant and Myrna Loy. Now at MGM, he was given the Hackett-Goodrich script and asked to rewrite it in a lighter, more positive, more humorous manner.

Walters wanted Frank Sinatra to play Kelly's friend in the film, as the two had worked well together in *Anchors Aweigh* a few years earlier. But Sinatra was busy with other projects, so Peter Lawford was hired. Cyd Charisse was then signed as Kelly's partner, who leaves to pursue a solo career, resulting in his connecting with Garland.

First, Gene Kelly sprained his ankle playing sports and had to drop out. Fearing the wrath of studio head Louis B. Mayer, Kelly claimed he hurt himself rehearsing a difficult dance step, and that's what the newspapers of the time reported. Kelly suggested Freed hire Fred Astaire to replace him.

Fred Astaire had done a few films for MGM already, but had been offscreen for about a year. Astaire was considering semi-retirement when he was contacted by Arthur Freed to take Gene Kelly's place. Attracted to the project not only by the prospect of working with Judy Garland, but also by the opportunity to perform some new Irving Berlin music, Astaire agreed to take the role, but only after speaking personally to Gene Kelly and making sure he was unable to do it. Not long afterward, Cyd Charisse was also injured, and was replaced by Ann Miller.

Ann Miller had, by this time, done a variety of supporting roles in movies, including Frank Capra's Best Picture Oscar winner *You Can't Take it With You* (1938), as well as films featuring everyone from the Marx Brothers and the Three Stooges, to Gene Autry and Glenn Ford. *Easter Parade* would be her first big MGM musical.

Set in 1912, Judy Garland plays Hannah Brown, a saloon performer who is noticed by Broadway star Don Hewes (Fred Astaire) whose partner, Nadine (Ann Miller), just left his act to go off as a single. Don hopes to groom Hannah into being his next partner, as he is impressed with her strong singing voice and stage manner. When they rehearse the next day, Hannah reveals her dancing is so poor that she actually has to stop and think as to which is her left foot and which is her right. He works with her, trying to make her another Nadine, and meanwhile his close friend Johnny (Peter Lawford) becomes attracted to Hannah. She, however, has eyes for her mentor Don. Eventually, Don realizes trying to make Hannah into Nadine is a mistake and starts devising routines that are more appropriate for his new partner. They plan to audition for the

Judy Garland and Fred Astaire were at their best in *Easter Parade*.

The Early Years—*Easter Parade* (1948)

Ziegfeld Follies, but Don is unsettled that the show's star is Nadine, and tells Hannah they don't belong in the same show. They do their own show, and during rehearsals when Hannah accuses Don of only seeing her as a work partner, it is eventually revealed that he is in love with her as much as she is with him. When Nadine suggests Don do one of their old numbers with Hannah watching, and Don reluctantly agrees, Hannah angrily walks out. However, they make up in time to join the Easter parade.

While the romantic plot is light and somewhat typical, Sidney Sheldon's rewrite made *Easter Parade* a very upbeat, positive film, and that experience found its way to the film's stars. Fred Astaire threw himself into the project with gusto, offering his carefree agility and pleasant manner to his role. Judy Garland's behavior was the polar opposite of what it had been on *The Pirate*. She clicked with every number, learned complicated routines with little rehearsal, and effectively matched the great Astaire step-for-step. Each of them had the chance to play comedy, drama, romance, and perform some truly great musical numbers. Although she had to go back to the set for *The Pirate* seventeen times for retakes, Garland maintained a happy attitude throughout the filming of *Easter Parade*, which turned out to be a tonic for the performer who had wanted to end her life only months before.

Frank Sinatra would likely have been a better choice as Johnny than Peter Lawford (Red Skelton was also briefly attached to the project). Lawford was a handsome man with a nice British voice, but lacked the charisma necessary for the character. Johnny was supposed to be attractive to both Nadine and Hannah. Ann Miller, however, was outstanding in the part of Nadine, allowing her the chance to play a formidable character and show off her magnificent tap dancing skills. Her character's haughty attitude and use of dogs as accessories, and the way her extravagant costumes contrast the more understated outfits worn by Hannah, are amusing traits. And her "Shakin' the Blues Away" is one of the highlights of *Easter Parade*, despite the fact that neither of the two leads participate in it.

Garland remained in good spirits throughout the production, so much so that it was brought in nearly $200,000 under budget and ahead of schedule. It was also an enormous hit at the box office, bringing in nearly three times its costs.

Irving Berlin, proud of his work, and of the subsequent film, did his best to help promote it, causing Lloyd L. Sloan's column in the *Los Angeles Evening News* to state:

The Films of Judy Garland

The Motion Picture Research Bureau which conducts polls among motion picture theatergoers announced recently that a survey shows Irving Berlin by a 57 per cent vote to be the nation's conception of the greatest living American composer of popular music. If such a vote were taken around MGM at the moment the result might be close to the 100 per cent mark. Mainly because of the "for free" work he has done press-agenting *Easter Parade* his Judy Garland-Fred Astaire picture Metro looking—naturally enough—at a picture in terms of cold cash sees the biggest dollar stimulation in a long time coming from *Easter Parade* which studio execs expect to be the best thing financially since *Gone with the Wind*. Because Berlin is putting so much effort and time into the promotion of *Easter* reports have gotten around that he owned a piece of the film that his share of the grosses would net him a million and a half dollars etc. Berlin denies all this. "The fact is," he has stated, "I will get no more than the $600000 I was originally paid for the package which became *Easter Parade*." This free cooperation has involved among other factors three transcontinental trips for Berlin to appear on radio programs plugging *Easter Parade* music and other journeys around the country for PA's and interviews. He recently appeared for interviews on four different network programs in one day. Berlin has given more of his time and effort to this film than for any previous celluloid venture including *Blue Skies* in which he did have a percentage interest in addition to his flat guarantee. All of which makes Mr. Berlin seem all the more fabulous in the eyes of cynical Hollywood where studios and people long ago gave up the idea of getting something for nothing.[61]

The success of *Easter Parade* went beyond the moviegoing public and made it to the critics as well. A review in the *San Francisco Examiner* stated:

In case you've ever taken time out to wonder just how nostalgic, or high styled, a musical can get, here we are bouncing up with the answer. It's *Easter Parade*. Personally, we're content to settle for this brilliantly produced Arthur Freed extravaganza, on every count. No exceptions! Not only do Fred Astaire, Judy Garland, Ann Miller and one Peter Lawford, turn in time cards that make exhilarating comedy-musical and dramatic sense, but the fanciful direction of Charles Walter makes this an entertainment jackpot.[62]

Fred Astaire and Judy Garland worked so well together that there were plans to reteam them in another film soon.

Upon completing *Easter Parade,* Judy Garland was one of many star cameos in the all-star musical drama *Words and Music*—a highly fictional story about the songwriting team of Richard Rogers and Lorenz Hart. Mickey Rooney played Hart, and performed with Garland, making it the last film in which the two former co-stars appeared together. Rooney had been MGM's biggest star in the late 1930s, but after a stint in the army, he returned to discover there was no place for him in the

The Early Years—*In the Good Old Summertime* (1949)

post-war era. Even though he kept making movies for over 60 more years, and garnered Oscar nominations and an Emmy, he never recaptured his pre-war superstardom. *Words and Music* was to be Rooney's last movie before leaving his longtime home of MGM and attempting independent deals, which was a disastrous move for his career. But it was fitting that his last film for the studio featured him in a musical number with Judy Garland.[63]

Words and Music also turned out to be the last big budget musical in which Judy Garland would appear. Despite her high spirits throughout the filming of *Easter Parade,* Garland's erratic behavior and continued issues made her a difficult investment. She was hereafter relegated to the less expensive, more relaxed Joe Pasternak productions, the first of which was a remake of an earlier MGM feature, *The Shop Around the Corner.*

In the Good Old Summertime

Directed by Robert Z. Leonard
Screenplay by Ivan Tors, Albert Hackett, and Frances Goodrich
  (based on the play by Miklós László)
Produced by Joe Pasternak
Cinematography by Harry Stradling
Film editing by Adrienne Fazan
Songs:
  "In the Good Old Summertime"; Music by George Evans; Lyrics by Ren Shields
  "Meet Me Tonight in Dreamland"; Music by Leo Friedman; Lyrics by Beth Slater Whitson
  "Put Your Arms Around Me, Honey (I Never Knew Any Girl Like You)"; Music by Albert von Tilzer; Lyrics by Junie McCree
  "Wait Till the Sun Shines, Nellie"; Music by Harry Von Tilzer; Lyrics by Andrew B. Sterling
  "Play That Barbershop Chord"; Written by Ballard MacDonald, William Tracey, and Lewis F. Muir
  "I Don't Care"; Music by Harry O. Sutton; Lyrics by Jean Lenox
  "Merry Christmas"; Music by Fred Spielman; Lyrics by Janice Torre
Cast: Judy Garland, Van Johnson, S.Z. Sakall, Spring Byington,

The Films of Judy Garland

Clinton Sundberg, Buster Keaton, Marcia Van Dyke, Lillian Bronson, Joan Wells, Charles Smith, George Boyce, Eddie Jackson, Joe Niemeyer, Chester Clute, Betty Arlen, James Gonzalez, William Bailey, Everett Glass, Jack Deery, Edward Biby, Joe Gilbert, William Forest, Mary Bayless, Antonio Filauri, Carli Elinor, Eula Guy, Clark Ross, Joi Lansing, Constance Purdy, Peggy Leon, Arthur Rosenstein, Carl Leviness, Anna Q. Nilsson, Jack Roth, Howard Mitchell, Josephine Whittel, Ralph Sanford, Bobby Valentine, Rhea Mitchell, and Liza Minnelli

MGM
Released July 29, 1949
102 minutes
Technicolor

After the success of *Easter Parade,* Judy Garland went from her guest spot in *Words and Music* into another big musical with Fred Astaire, *The Barkleys of Broadway.* While the experience on *Easter Parade* was a positive one, and Garland gamely tried to maintain the grueling rehearsal schedule for *The Barkleys of Broadway,* it was just too much for her. Her reliance on prescription medication and general manner simply didn't mesh with a lifestyle that went from one hard schedule to another. Even her physician contacted Arthur Freed and recommended she be replaced. MGM hired Ginger Rogers to reteam with Fred Astaire for the first time in nine years, making *The Barkleys of Broadway* a huge hit.

Joe Pasternak was preparing a remake of the 1940 MGM feature *The Shop Around the Corner,* with color and music. He originally planned to cast Frank Sinatra and Gloria DeHaven, and then settled on Sinatra and June Allyson. However, Allyson had just adopted a child and was taking some time off, and Sinatra's latest MGM feature, *The Kissing Bandit,* was a flop. With the availability of Judy Garland, Pasternak thought he could pair her with Gene Kelly for this film. But it was decided that Sinatra only achieved decent box office when he was in a film with Kelly, so the two of them were placed in Stanley Donen's *On the Town* for Arthur Freed. Garland, however, was available, and a charming comedy with a few musical numbers was just the project she needed.

Van Johnson was eventually cast opposite Judy Garland. One of the most popular leading men on the MGM lot, Johnson had proven himself to be able to play both comedy and drama with equal aplomb. A younger man was planned to play his rival for Garland's affections, but at one point this actor would have to do a pratfall as trained by the great Buster Keaton. Keaton is remembered today as one of the top comedians and

The Early Years—*In the Good Old Summertime* (1949)

filmmakers of the silent era, but he had had a series of personal and professional struggles since that time, including being fired by MGM in 1933. He was now back at the studio as a gagman. Pasternak realized that only Keaton could perform the physical stunt needed for an important scene in the film, so it was decided he would play the role, despite being much older than Johnson or Garland. It would be his first appearance in an MGM picture since *What! No Beer?* in 1933.

Back in the 1930s, Joe Pasternak hired a Hungarian actor to appear at Universal. The actor, S.Z. Sakall, had enjoyed success in German films, but fled that country when the Nazis started taking over. After coming to America, he was hired by Pasternak and enjoyed success at Universal before going over to Warner Brothers, where he made his name with small parts in big movies, most notably *Casablanca*. Pasternak believed nobody other than Sakall could play the role of the shopkeeper in this movie, so he arranged for MGM to borrow the actor from Warner Brothers. The cast was rounded out with Spring Byington, Clinton Sundberg, and violin virtuoso Marica Van Dyke. Several titles were considered before Pasternak decided on *In the Good Old Summertime*. Robert Z. Leonard was hired to direct.

Set at the outset of the 20th century, Judy Garland plays Veronica

Van Johnson and Judy Garland co-starred in *The Good Old Summertime*.

The Films of Judy Garland

Fisher, a lonely woman whose only happiness is via letters she receives from a male pen pal with whom she is carrying on a romance through the postal service. They initially began writing to share intellectual ideas, but soon became romantically attracted to each other's words despite never having seen one another. Veronica goes to get a job at a music shop, but first has a run-in with a young man who bumps into her as he is walking down the street reading and not paying attention to where he is going. Once Veronica gets in the store, she sees that the man, Andy Larkin (Van Johnson), is the head salesman, while the proprietor, Otto Oberkugen, isn't hiring. Andy and Otto have been fighting over an expensive harp that Otto purchased to sell in the store. Andy thinks it was a bad idea, believing nobody plays harps and it will never sell. While still in the store, Veronica plays the harp and sings while a customer is deciding on some sheet music, and ends up selling the woman the harp. A pleased Otto hires her, much to Andy's chagrin. Of course, neither Veronica nor Andy realize that they are the pen pals that have been writing to each other, but, despite that, their initial conflict still grows into an attraction.

In the Good Old Summertime was another happy assignment for Judy Garland, and once again her cooperation resulted in the movie coming in under budget and ahead of its production deadline. Unlike Arthur Freed, who preferred to hire songwriters to compose some new numbers for his films, Joe Pasternak liked scoring period pieces with appropriate songs from the era. As the only actor who sang in the movie, Judy Garland was comfortable and happy with the vintage selections and pre-recorded them without incident over an easy two-day period.

Buster Keaton seems miscast as the rival for Garland's affections, being nearly 30 years older, but they present him as a quaint, harmless little man who finds her pretty but doesn't really believe he has much of a chance. Keaton supervised the physical gags in the film, including when Van Johnson and Judy Garland first connect. He knocks off her hat, tries to put it back on, and goes through a series of motions that are clearly Keaton's influence. His pratfall happens when he is delivering Otto's priceless Stradivarius to him on stage, but stumbles and destroys it. While the narrative reveals that it was a replacement (Andy loaned the actual one to a female friend for an audition), the fall itself is something only Keaton could have pulled off as effectively and amusingly.

In the Good Old Summertime features Judy Garland at her most charming and appealing, exhibiting her flair for comedy through an appealing screen character. One song that she filmed, "Last Night When We Were Young," was cut from the film before release, but Garland kept

The Early Years—*In the Good Old Summertime* (1949)

Buster Keaton joined Judy Garland In *The Good Old Summertime*, appearing in his first MGM movie since 1933.

it in her repertoire for years, and the recording for this film still exists as well as the actual footage shot for the movie. This film is also notable as being Liza Minnelli's film debut. The three-year-old appeared as the child at the end of the film.

Garland is lovely in this movie, and performs each song beautifully. "I Don't Care" is maybe the most memorable number. The Technicolor in this film is also really bright and pretty and suits the period setting well. The film does tone down a lot of the original material from *The Shop Around the Corner*, however, in favor of lighter fare, most notably the shop owner's wife's affair and his subsequent suicide attempt.

In the Good Old Summertime was yet another big hit for Judy Garland, and for MGM, grossing more than double its production costs at the box office. And because Garland worked so well on her last two projects, the studio felt she could effectively perform in another big budget musical they had ready for her. She reported to the set of Arthur Freed's musical production of *Annie Get Your Gun* in the title role of Annie Oakley, made famous on Broadway by the bombastic Ethel Merman. Garland recorded all of the songs for the soundtrack and then prepared to act in the movie.

Arthur Freed hired Busby Berkeley as director, believing his vision was best for the production. However, Garland and Berkeley had conflicted often on past projects, and she used her clout to have him removed from the film *Girl Crazy*. While *In the Good Old Summertime* was a pleasant experience where Garland was met with patience, support, and understanding, Busby Berkeley was once again very demanding, pushing the frail actress well past her emotional limit. Garland wanted to play the character in her own way, while Berkeley wanted a more boisterous portrayal as Ethel Merman had done on stage. Garland complained directly to Louis B. Mayer, and Berkeley was taken off the project and replaced by Charles Walters.

Despite this, Judy Garland's attempt to maintain focus on *Annie Get Your Gun* was still too difficult. Underweight, addicted to prescription drugs, and wallowing in depression over her continued difficult marriage to Vincente Minnelli, Garland missed several days of filming and showed up late for others. After several warnings, her contract was suspended, and she was removed from the film, to be replaced later by Betty Hutton. Garland then went to Boston and was hospitalized for several weeks in an effort to regain her strength. But there was some discussion at the studio as to whether Judy Garland, one of MGM's most popular stars, was now too much of a risk.

Summer Stock

Directed by Charles Walters
Screenplay by George Wells and Sy Gomberg (from a story by Gomberg)

The Early Years—*Summer Stock* (1950)

Produced by Joe Pasternak
Cinematography by Robert Planck
Film editing by Albert Akst
Songs:
  "All for You"; Written by Saul Chaplin
  "Dig-Dig-Dig-Dig for Your Dinner"; Music by Harry Warren; Lyrics by Mack Gordon
  "Friendly Star"; Music by Harry Warren; Lyrics by Mack Gordon
  "Get Happy":Music by Harold Arlen; Lyrics by Ted Koehler
  "(Howdy Neighbor) Happy Harvest"; Music by Harry Warren; Lyrics by Mack Gordon
  "Heavenly Music"; Written by Saul Chaplin
  "If You Feel Like Singing, Sing"; Music by Harry Warren: Lyrics by Mack Gordon
  "Mem'ry Island"; Music by Harry Warren; Lyrics by Mack Gordon
  "You Wonderful You"; Music by Harry Warren: Lyric by Jack Brooks and Saul Chaplin
Cast: Judy Garland, Gene Kelly, Phil Silvers, Gloria DeHaven, Eddie Bracken, Marjorie Main, Ray Collins, Nita Bieber, Carleton Carpenter, Hans Conried, Erville Alderson, Paul E. Burns, Jack Daley, A. Cameron Grant, Almira Sessions, Jean Adcock, Bridget Carr, Jeanne Coyne, Joan Dale, Johnny Duncan, Carol Haney, Betty Hannon, Dickie Humphreys, Rena Lenart, Arthur Loew, Jr., Don Powell, Elynne Ray, Marilyn Reiss, Joe Roach, Albert Ruiz, Jimmy Thompson, Joanne Tree, Dorothy Tuttle, Carol West, George Bunny, Nora Bush, Roy Butler, Michael Chapin, Eddie Dunn, Luigi Faccuito, Slim Gaut, Dick John Stone, Al Kunde, Anny Kunde, Henry Sylvester, Glen Walters, Bert May, Teddy Infuhr, Jack Gargan, and Margaret Bert
MGM
Released August 5, 1950
108 minutes
Technicolor

After spending six weeks at the Peter Brent Bingham hospital in Boston for what we would today call "rehab," Judy Garland returned to MGM. She stopped to visit the *Annie Get Your Gun* set, and when she was cheerfully greeted by Betty Hutton, her replacement on the film, she let loose a series of profanities and was escorted from the set. While the two of them later reconciled, and Garland admitted she thought Hutton did better in the role than she could have done herself, Hutton never forgot how hurt she'd been.

The Films of Judy Garland

It was decided that Garland would be placed in another Joe Pasternak production where she would be given the space, love, and patience she needed in her condition. *Summer Stock* was an attempt to return to the sort of musical she used to make with Mickey Rooney, where a group of performers put on a show in a barn. Pasternak wanted Rooney to co-star, but, he had left MGM by this time, after listening to bad advice from his agent-manager, and was appearing in indie productions like the racecar drama *The Big Wheel* (1949), and the film noir *Quicksand* (1950). Pasternak then sought Gene Kelly as co-star.

By this time, Kelly had enjoyed not only greater popularity, but his latest movie, *On the Town*, allowed him a lot of creative input and it redefined dance on film. A smaller film like *Summer Stock* was actually something of a comedown for Gene Kelly, but he agreed to do the film because of his continued loyalty to Judy Garland. Pasternak hired a lot of Garland's friends for the film, including Charles Walters as director, and comedian Phil Silvers, whom she adored, and who had worked very successfully with Gene Kelly in the Columbia musical *Cover Girl* (1944). Other friends like Marjorie Main, Gloria DeHaven, and Eddie Bracken were added to the cast.

Filming began in October 1949 and after twenty days of production, Garland had already missed six. She was reprimanded by MGM and went to Louis B. Mayer and asked to be taken off the production. Garland was concerned she might lose the good health she had just achieved through rehab. Mayer refused, believing another situation like *Annie Get Your Gun* would destroy her. He convinced her to return to the production. Charles Walters would later recall:

> Gene took her left arm and I took her right one, and between us, we literally tried to keep her on her feet. But it wasn't easy. Emotionally she was at her lowest ebb. Physically she was pretty unsure of herself as well. There were even times when we had to nail the scenery down and provide her with supports so she wouldn't fall over. Once, I remember, she had to walk up a few steps, and she couldn't do it. So I had to cheat the shot, and shoot the scene from a different angle. The whole experience was a ghastly, hideous nightmare which, happily, is a blur in my memory.[64]

Judy Garland had gained some healthy weight while away, and if this had been an Arthur Freed production, she would likely have been placed on a crash diet. Fortunately, Joe Pasternak required no weight loss, thus eliminating at least some of the pressure Garland placed upon herself. She gamely struggled through the production, buoyed by the patience and support of the producer, director, cast, and crew.

The Early Years—*Summer Stock* (1950)

Judy Garland plays Jane Falbury, a farm owner whose crops have been performing poorly for so long that her farmhands have all quit due to her inability to pay them. Her sister Abigail, an actress, descends upon the farm with an entire musical troupe, planning to put on a show in the barn. Jane is upset at first and against the idea, but eventually agrees to the arrangement on the condition that the show people will chip in and help with the chores. They agree to do so, but have no idea how the work is done. The show's producer, Joe Ross (Gene Kelly), is engaged to Abigail, but soon falls for Jane. Jane is engaged to timid hometown boy Orville, who is controlled by his pushy father (Ray Collins). Abigail suddenly leaves the show and goes off to New York with a hammy actor (Hans Conried), believing he can advance her career. Joe asks Jane to step in and play Abigail's part, and she rises to the occasion.

Despite Garland's physical, mental, and emotional challenges during the production of *Summer Stock*, she turns in a wonderful performance. Highlights include her anguish when the show people

Marjorie Main, Gloria DeHaven, Gene Kelly, and Judy Garland in *Summer Stock*.

accidentally wreck an expensive tractor, her dry sarcasm toward the inability of the show people to do simple farm tasks, her singing, and her dancing. Judy Garland turns in one of her career-best performances.

Regarding her singing, other studies have pointed out that Garland's singing performances were in transition at this time. The sweeter sounds of past films were evolving into the more forceful, dramatic presentations that would be found in later films like *A Star Is Born*. Her dancing is perhaps best exhibited in the "Portland Fancy" number, where the traditional style is supplanted by a swing version, with Garland matching all of Gene Kelly's complicated steps. The "Portland Fancy" number does a great job of advancing the story and Jane and Joe's relationship. Their dancing is a confrontation, an argument, but by the end of the number they appear to at least begrudgingly respect each other. Scenes like this make it difficult to believe that Garland was suffering with a myriad of personal issues throughout the filming.

A slimmed-down Garland performed her *Get Happy* number two months after production wrapped.

The Early Years—*Summer Stock* (1950)

Production had concluded for two months when it was realized that the film didn't have a show-stopping solo number for Judy Garland. Plans were made for Garland to return to perform the song "Get Happy" and insert that scene into the movie. She agreed, but by that time she had gone on a bit of a health regimen and lost 20 pounds. Because she is noticeably slimmer during the "Get Happy" number, other studies have speculated that the scene had been cut from an earlier movie. No, the "Get Happy" number was exclusively filmed for *Summer Stock*. Garland's rendition of "Get Happy" became not only one of her most famous numbers but one of the most well-known scenes from any movie musical, and her costume, consisting of the top half of a tuxedo, is now iconic.

Much of the comedy in *Summer Stock* comes from the theatrical performers trying to adapt to farm chores, with Phil Silvers having ample opportunity to do his "glad-to-see-ya" early film persona that sustained him until he found a new career in television as Ernie Bilko on his own *Phil Silvers Show*. He gets to perform a one-on-one number with Gene Kelly, because when it was time to film the "Heavenly Music" number, Judy Garland, who was supposed to be in it, didn't show up to work.

Along with Silvers, Eddie Bracken is quite amusing as the stammering, unsure Orville, who is fiercely guided by his blustery, overbearing father, played by a happy, scenery-chewing Ray Collins. And, although he is decidedly the villain of the movie as the ham actor who steals Abigail from the show, Hans Conried is a master of comical conceit. Finally, Marjorie Main, as Jane's loyal cook and housekeeper, is at her rustic best. Marjorie did this film just as her career-defining Ma and Pa Kettle film series with Percy Kilbride was getting started.

Everything about *Summer Stock* worked effectively, but the film did go over budget due to Garland's absences and breakdowns, none of which were evident in her performance. Despite this, *Summer Stock* was a commercial hit and a critical favorite. However, in June 1950, a couple of months before *Summer Stock* was released, Garland made international headlines due to a suicide attempt. There was concern that this would alienate her public, but in September when she quietly attended a screening of *Summer Stock* at New York's Capitol Theater, she was spotted in the audience as the film concluded, and received cheers from the moviegoers, who yelled, "We love you, Judy!" It buoyed her spirits considerably.

MGM next wanted Judy Garland to co-star with Fred Astaire in

Eddie Bracken, Phil Silvers, Gene Kelly, and Judy Garland.

Royal Wedding, replacing June Allyson, who dropped out because she was pregnant with her second child. Charles Walters was set to direct, but when Garland replaced Allyson, he asked producer Arthur Freed to remove him from the project. He couldn't see himself going through another production like *Summer Stock*, despite how well it turned out. Stanley Donen was hired as director, but it soon became apparent that Garland was in no shape to work on the film. Only agreeing to work half days during rehearsals, Garland kept calling in sick as soon as production began. This caused Freed to remove her from the production and cast Jane Powell in her place.

Contrary to what has been written elsewhere, Judy Garland was not fired from MGM. She asked for, and received, her release. After

The Early Years—*Summer Stock* (1950)

15 years of being overworked, Garland just didn't want to make movies anymore.

Judy Garland's marriage to Vincente Minnelli ended in 1951 due to her having an affair with Sid Luft, who became her manager, and, in 1952, her third husband. It was Luft who convinced Garland to return to live performances to reconnect with people. *Summer Stock* turned out to be the last movie Judy Garland would make for four years.

Back on Stage
1951–1954

No longer under contract to MGM, and not pursuing movie opportunities anywhere, Judy Garland first returned to the public eye via Bing Crosby's popular radio show. Bing invited her to appear on the new season's premiere show on October 11, 1950. Her suicide attempt in June had made headlines, and while the spontaneous audience reaction when she was spotted at a New York movie theater in September had lifted her spirits, she was still very nervous about going on Bing's show. Hal Kanter, one of Bing's writers, recalled:

> She was standing in the wings of it trembling with fear. She was almost hysterical. She said, "I cannot go out there because they're all gonna be looking to see if there are scars, and it's gonna be terrible." Bing said "What's going on?" and I told him what happened and he walked out on stage and he said: "We got a friend here, she's had a little trouble recently. You probably heard about it—everything is fine now, she needs our love. She needs our support. She's here—let's give it to her, OK? Here's Judy." And she came out, and that place went crazy. And she just blossomed.[1]

Garland subsequently made a total of eight appearances on Bing Crosby's radio show during the 1950–1951 season, and their success gave her the confidence to explore a tour of live performances.

The plan was to showcase Garland in a special show at the New York Palace Theater with the theme of bringing vaudeville back to the Palace. However, before this happened, Garland wanted to try out her act in some venues overseas, so she took a tour of the UK. Garland had an enormous fan base in England, so her first live concert was at the London Palladium, where she performed concerts for nearly a month (April 9–May 5, 1951). It was a huge success, and she was in fine form, belting out classic songs from her movie career to a packed house each night.

Garland then spent two successful weeks at the Empire Theater in Glasgow, Scotland, followed by a week of concerts in Manchester,

Back on Stage

Garland maintained a public presence via her appearances on Bing Crosby's radio show.

England, and another week performing in Liverpool. She finished out the summer with concerts in Dublin, Ireland, and Birmingham, England.

Beginning in October 1951 and extending until February 1952, Judy Garland did her "Back to Vaudeville" show at the Palace in New York. It had originally been scheduled for nine weeks but was extended to fourteen due to demands for tickets. Garland sang such noted songs as "Call the Papers," "On the Town," "Judy at the Palace Medley," "Rock-A-Bye Your Baby," "Love Is Sweeping the Country," "Judy's Olio" ("You Made Me Love You"/"For Me and My Gal"/"The Boy Next Door"/"The Trolley Song"), "Get Happy," "A Couple of Swells," and "Over the Rainbow." The suddenly tireless performer was doing as many as 13 performances per week, with a

The Films of Judy Garland

week off in November to avoid succumbing to exhaustion. She also took off a few days during the Christmas holidays. Her final night at the Palace, on February 24, 1952, was recorded and has been available as a record, tape, CD, etc., for decades. This triumphant return to the American stage culminated with Garland being given a special Tony Award for her achievement.

There are those who believe Judy Garland's true talents were presented in live performances, not in motion pictures. Some believe her movies are only as important to her career as, say, Frank Sinatra's or Elvis Presley's—a sideline to what defined her true career. Well, there are entire books written, including by this author, that celebrate the screen work of Sinatra, and of Presley, as being a significant part of their show business repertoire, but it is true that they are secondary to their stage and recording careers. Each of these men was already a leading star when they made their first movies. This is not the case for Judy Garland. While she began on stage with her sisters, Garland's movie career is what made her famous. This allowed for her to enjoy a successful stage career. However, what must be pointed out is that Judy Garland's best work might be what she did on stage. She was truly a magnificent presence when performing live in concert, her strong voice soaring through even the largest and most imposing venues.

After some time off, Garland returned to the stage with the Los Angeles Philharmonic from April 21–May 18, 1952. She made three more appearances on Bing Crosby's radio show during this same period, and then appeared for about a month at the Curran Theater in San Francisco, which would be Garland's last engagement for her vaudeville show. She married Sid Luft on June 8, 1952, after which she took a break so the two could honeymoon. In late

Garland triumphantly returned to the stage.

Back on Stage—*A Star Is Born* (1954)

October 1952, it was Garland's turn to come to Bing Crosby's rescue when Bing's wife Dixie was seriously ill and near death. Crosby needed time off to be at her bedside, and Garland agreed to take over the radio show in the meantime. Then on November 21, 1952, Judy Garland gave birth to her second child, Lorna Luft.

As a result of her second child's birth, Garland was less active in 1953. She did some radio, including starring in the radio play *Lady in the Dark*, and on April 29, she headlined at the bluegrass festival in Kentucky as part of Derby Week, closing her performance with a rendition of "My Old Kentucky Home." While in Kentucky, Garland visited the Shriner's hospital to meet with, and sign autographs for, the patients.

As aforementioned, Garland married Sid Luft in June 1952. Later that summer, the couple formed their own production company, Transcona, and met with Warner Brothers about Garland returning to motion pictures. So, Judy Garland, considered "washed up" in movies only a couple years earlier, was back at work on her first motion picture in four years. It turned out to be what many consider to be the greatest performance in her entire screen career.

A Star Is Born

Directed by George Cukor
Screenplay by Moss Hart (based on the 1937 screenplay by Dorothy Parker, Alan Campbell, and Robert Carson, which itself was based on a story by Carson and William A. Wellman)
Produced by Sidney Luft
Cinematography by Sam Leavitt
Film editing by Folmar Blangsted
Songs:
    "Gotta Have Me Go with You"; Music by Harold Arlen; Lyrics by Ira Gershwin
    "The Man That Got Away"; Music by Harold Arlen; Lyrics by Ira Gershwin
    "Here's What I'm Here For"; Music by Harold Arlen; Lyrics by Ira Gershwin
    "Lose That Long Face"; Music by Harold Arlen; Lyrics by Ira Gershwin

The Films of Judy Garland

"Someone at Last"; Music by Harold Arlen; Lyrics by Ira Gershwin

"It's a New World"; Music by Harold Arlen; Lyrics by Ira Gershwin

"Trinidad Coconut Oil Shampoo"; Music by Harold Arlen" Lyrics by Ira Gershwin

"Born in a Trunk"; Music by Roger Edens; Lyrics by Leonard Gershe

"Swanee"; Music by George Gershwin; Lyrics by Irving Caesar

Cast: Judy Garland, James Mason, Jack Carson, Charles Bickford, Tommy Noonan, Lucy Marlow, Amanda Blake, Irving Bacon, Frank Ferguson, Hazel Shermet, James Brown, Stephen Wyman, Frank Wilcox, Rudolph Anders, Don Beddoe, Willis Bouchey, Blythe Daley, Fred Kelsey, Franklyn Farnum, George Fisher, Nacho Galindo, Grady Sutton, Michael Hall, Dick Simmons, Ray Heindorf, Nancy Kulp, Percy Helton, Olin Howland, Bob Jellison, Emerson Treacy, Henry Kulky, Barbara Pepper, Arthur Space, Frank Puglia, Jean Willes, Harry Seymour, Patrick Sexton, Joan Shawlee, Valerie Vernon, Geraldine Wall, Dub Taylor, Charles Watts, Richard Webb, Eric Wilton, Mary Young, Leon Alton, Gertrude Astor, John Saxon, Ruth Brady, Paul Brinegar, Sheila Bromley, Paul Bryar, Kathryn Card, Spencer Chan, Chick Chandler, Lauren Chapin, Heinie Conklin, Eddie Dew, Bess Flowers, Almeda Fowler, Joseph Glick, Wilton Graff, Charles Halton, Joseph Hamilton, Louis Jean Heydt, Dick Johnstone, Jack Kenney, Carl M. Leviness, Carey Loftin, Mae Marsh, Strother Martin, Louis Mason, Philo McCullough, Don McKay, Joseph Mell, Harold Miller, Mort Mills, Charles Morton, Jack Mower, Tom Nolan, Barry Norton, Rony Nyman, William H. O'Brien, Monty O'Grady, Pat O'Malley, Leonard Penn, Jack Pepper, Grandon Rhodes, Leoda Richards, Lotus Robb, Riza Royce, Loretta Russell, Reginald Simpson, Robert Stevenson, Wayne Taylor, Al Thompson, Ted Thorpe, Dale Van Sickel, Ralph Volkie, Louis Tomei, Eileen Stevens, Buddy Spencer, Bobby Sailes, Dick Ryan, Murray Pollack, Mel Pogue, Patrick Miller, Jack McCoy, Ila McAvoy, Nina Matthews, Gloria Lewin, and Allen Kramer

Warner Brothers

Released October 16, 1954

182 minutes (premiere), 154 minutes (general release), 176 minutes (restoration)

Technicolor

Back on Stage—*A Star Is Born* (1954)

In 1932, RKO released a movie entitled *What Price Hollywood?* about a waitress who is discovered by a famous, but drunken, Hollywood director and put in movies. Her career rises while his plummets. The movie was directed by George Cukor. In 1937, David O. Selznick wanted to produce a movie called *A Star Is Born*, which is a different story but the same concept and framework. Cukor was asked to direct but turned the project down, believing it to be too close to the *What Price Hollywood?* film. William Wellman took over the direction, and the stars were Janet Gaynor and Fredric March. The movie became a big hit and lived on as a timeless classic.

After Judy Garland's career, and spirits, were buoyed by her successful concert performances, she and Sid Luft explored a return to movies. Sid made a deal for his and Garland's production company to produce nine films for Warner Brothers, the first being a big budget musical version of the 1937 version of *A Star Is Born*. Sid wanted Cukor to direct, and made a lunch appointment with him. When Cukor met Luft, before he even sat down, he said that if this was for him to direct a movie with Garland, the answer was already yes. He didn't particularly care what the story was.

George Cukor had never directed Judy Garland. The closest he came was when he spent a short time on *The Wizard of Oz* and changed her look from the concept created by original director Richard Thorpe to the presentation of Dorothy that we now know.

Judy Garland was already quite familiar with playing the female lead in *A Star Is Born*. She and Walter Pidgeon

Judy Garland returned to movies after a four-year absence.

had actually co-starred in a radio version of the story back in 1942. It was non-musical, just a straight drama, but still a good training ground for the movie she would make a dozen years later.

The official announcement for *A Star Is Born* happened in September 1952, with production scheduled to begin about a year later. Garland gave birth to her second child, daughter Lorna Luft, in November 1952. Then, in early January 1953, Garland's mother, Ethel Gumm, died. Although there had been serious conflicts between the two over the

Garland and husband Sid Luft formed their own production company.

Back on Stage—*A Star Is Born* (1954)

years, and they were estranged, Garland broke down and wept upon receiving the news.

In April 1953, Garland recorded some new tracks for an album to be released by Columbia, with which she had recently entered into a contract. Columbia would also have the album rights to the *A Star Is Born* soundtrack. However, as it turned out, these albums would be the only Judy Garland projects released by that company.

A Star Is Born is the familiar story of a leading actor named Norman Maine who is secure in his stardom and takes advantage of his privileges to the point of upsetting the studio and the press agent, who has to get him out of trouble and cover for him. He meets beautiful, naturally talented Esther Blodgett, and uses his influence to get her in movies. Impressed with her natural talent, the studio promotes Esther and gives her the stage name Vicki Lester, and her stardom soars as Norman's spirals downhill due to his excesses and the fact that his audience has grown tired of him. While the Wellman film presented Norman as a

James Mason was chosen as Garland's leading man in *A Star Is Born*.

tragic figure, the Cukor version makes Norman a more egocentric type whose reaction to his situation is more volatile in its brooding.

Cary Grant was first asked to play Norman Maine in this new version, but he felt he was not right for the part. A variety of interesting actors were considered—including Richard Burton, Tyrone Power, Laurence Olivier, even Marlon Brando—each of whom would have offered a very significant take on the role. The part of Norman eventually went to James Mason, who explores the character's insecurities and simmering anger brilliantly.

Garland's official first day of work on *A Star Is Born* was in August 1953, but that initially meant recording her songs, costume fittings, makeup tests, and choreography. Actual filming began in October.

For the most part, Garland cooperated on the project and worked hard at playing a complex dramatic character and singing powerful, heartfelt songs like "The Man That Got Away," and the multi-layered epic "Born in a Trunk," which effectively offers the character's backstory. There were times when Garland's insecurities set in, when she would be haunted by how much was riding on the success of this project. At one point when she arrived three hours late, and then wouldn't come out of her dressing room, Cukor went in and asked, "Is anything wrong?" He then burst out laughing at the absurdity of his question and Garland joined him, saying, "This is the story of my life. I'm about to shoot myself and I'm asked if there's anything wrong."[2]

There was more than one instance in *A Star Is Born* where Garland had to dig rather deeply and play an emotional scene where Esther was a wreck. Her growing stresses over Norman's volatile behavior and his habit of going missing for days at a time caused the emotionally overwrought Esther to lash out on several occasions. Garland asked Cukor, "Do I really let myself go?" He said yes. Her performances were magnificent in these instances, and at one point Cukor approached her after she did an especially emotional scene and stated, "Judy, that was just glorious! My blood froze!" Still teary-eyed from the scene, Garland quipped, "You should come out to the house, George, I do that every afternoon!"[3]

The difficulties on *A Star Is Born* came less from Judy Garland's behavior and more from the constant interference of Jack Warner, who had concerns about the film's budget, its length, Sid Luft's lack of experience as a producer, and other situations. After a month of shooting, Warner insisted everything done so far be scrapped and reshot in Cinemascope. This was a very new process to make motion pictures bigger and grander than what could be found on television. The popularity of

Back on Stage—*A Star Is Born* (1954)

the small screen was growing, and theater owners were concerned about people staying home. Ideas like widescreen movies and 3-D productions were experiments in the early 1950s. While Cinemascope eventually became the norm in 1953, it seemed like something of a novelty. It might benefit outdoor location productions like westerns, but Cukor felt his character-driven movie would not benefit from it at all. In fact, he felt Cinemascope could hinder his presentation. Warner was adamant, so the completed scenes were reshot.

This was George Cukor's first movie in color, first musical, and now his first using the widescreen process. He made the best use of all, darkening the edges of the widescreen shot so the viewer's eyes would be drawn to the characters.

Despite any disruptions or interruptions, George Cukor was creating a cinematic masterpiece. Judy Garland was turning in what may be her career-best performance. James Mason was effectively walking the fine line between likeable leading man and volatile antagonist.

Another standout is Jack Carson as press agent Matt Libby. Unlike the dismissive cynic played so well by Lionel Stander in the 1937 movie, Carson played the agent as someone who seethed with hatred for Norman and was tired of covering for his excesses, angered by his connection to a nice girl like Esther, and delighted with his fall. When he reveals his feelings to Norman once he no longer has to cover for him, Norman states, "Let's not forget we're friends," cluelessly believing that Libby genuinely cared and wasn't just doing a job. Carson practically spits his final lines to Norman, before punching him to the floor when the failed actor tries to start a fight.

A Star Is Born premiered in September 1954 at just over three hours, and it was unanimous among premiere audiences and critics that Judy Garland was back. The film was applauded as an epic classic. Garland made the cover of *Life* magazine for the first time since the release of *Meet Me in St. Louis*. However, just as the movie was starting to play theaters, Warner Brothers decided it was too long, and believed if it was cut, they could have one more show time per theater, and garner more box office to offset the production costs. The studio insisted the film be returned by exhibitors, and then randomly cut the film down to 154 minutes and put it back into general release. George Cukor angrily stated that he could have trimmed the film more effectively, but the studio argued that he had gone on to his next project and they didn't believe he'd be available to re-edit the movie. What was left was a film that seemed a bit disjointed in spots and was hardly the epic classic it once had been. Still, Garland's terrific acting stood out.

The Films of Judy Garland

Because of all the trouble, Garland and Luft's production company made no more movies for Warner Brothers, and Garland was once again off movie screens, this time for seven years. But she was pleased with the fact that she got through the film successfully, and was lauded for her fine performance despite the butchering of the film by the studio. Judy Garland was nominated for an Oscar, which she lost to Grace Kelly for *The Country Girl*. But Garland had done what she set out to do—carry a big budget musical film as its star and turn in a fine, committed performance.

The original cut of *A Star Is Born* was rescued in the early 1980s by Ronald Haver, a film historian who signaled the interest in film preservation with his work in restoring *A Star Is Born*. According to an article in *American Film Magazine*:

> When I was working at the Los Angeles County Museum of Art, with archivist David Shepard, we decided to show *A Star Is Born* as part of a Cukor retrospective, and to accompany it with a brochure, using stills and script extracts, to show exactly what had been cut. Cukor lent us his script and his complete collection of stills from the film, and we were able to finally itemize just exactly what had been taken out, and assess the damage to the story. Rudi Fehr, then vice-president in charge of post-production, told me that he had his people go through their records and storage vaults and that they turned up nothing. Evidently, the cut sections had been kept for several months and then destroyed, a common practice at most major studios. I was convinced that if I could get free, unlimited access to the studio vaults, a careful combing through all those thousands of cans of film would turn up the footage, possibly in mismarked cans.[4]

Haver's article continued to explain how he discovered the missing footage and the soundtrack materials, and effectively restored what had been missing. Haver's work resulted in the restored film as we see it today, but it isn't exactly the original, uncut version; he never found all of the missing footage, so stills of the scenes were spliced in where they belonged with the audio playing over them. Sadly, while George Cukor was excited about the project, he passed away the day before the restored film premiered on January 25, 1983. Ronald Haver died in 1993.

A Star Is Born was a triumph for Judy Garland, even though she didn't profit by it as a producer. After the money spent to switch to Cinemascope, call back the released prints to be re-edited, and other such expenses, *A Star Is Born* did not recoup its costs.

Returning to the Concert Stage

Judy Garland could not be in attendance at the Oscars when she was nominated for *A Star Is Born* because she had just given birth to her third child, and first son, Joseph Luft. But soon she was able to return to live performances and continued through the 1950s to pursue this new and highly successful venture.

At first, Garland investigated some opportunities in television. After a successful 1955 broadcast of *Ford Star Jubilee,* telecast in color, Garland and Luft signed a contract with CBS for more specials. They did another in 1956, but despite that one's success, the network disagreed with Garland and Luft on some format issues, and their relationship with CBS ended.

Returning to the concert stage, one of Garland's most successful performances was a four-week gig at the New Frontier Hotel in Las Vegas for $55,000 per week. Her powerful voice failed her and she contracted laryngitis. On one night, Jerry Lewis filled in for her, performing while Garland watched on stage from a wheelchair. Lewis recalled for the author:

> Dean and I had just broken up, and I didn't know what would happen to either of us. I didn't know if the public would accept me on my own. They loved Martin and Lewis as a unit, a team, and we broke up and took that away from them. Well, Sid Luft called and asked me to fill in for Judy. I was afraid, but he talked me into it. He said, "Judy has faith in you." That's all I needed to hear. So, I put together an act, doing comedy and a couple songs I knew. One of them was "Rock-a-bye Your Baby with a Dixie Melody," which was an old Al Jolson tune I loved. I hadn't sung alone on stage since I was 5! And here I was at 30 re-starting my career. Well, the place went nuts. My wife talked me into making "Rock-a-bye" a record, and it actually became a Top Ten hit. After that I had the confidence to continue on my own. I never forgot Sid and Judy for that.[1]

After that night, Garland continued her concerts, which remained so successful that her appearance was extended for a week.

The Films of Judy Garland

Garland continued throughout the 1950s turning in magnificent, highly successful concert performances, including a return to the Palace Theater in New York. Then in 1959, she was hospitalized with acute hepatitis which was so severe that the doctors told her she likely had no more than five years to live, and that she would never sing again. However, Garland recovered over several months of rest, and in August 1960 she returned to the Palladium in London for another successful series of concerts. Her voice was used in the 1960 film *Pepe*, an all-star attempt to bring Mexican comedy star Cantinflas to American screens. By all accounts, Garland was now in a comfortable place in her life, with health, success, and happiness.

While in London in January 1961, Garland was interviewed by syndicated columnist Tom Reedy, who assessed her situation:

> Judy Garland's little bunny nose is wrinkling up again with the joy of living. She's put away the pills. Mealtime is just that. Nobody is counting the calories. There are no studio spies saying do this, do that, don't don't don't. "I'm free" says the girl who sang her way into the hearts of millions of American film fans over a career just short of a quarter century. She said it like someone released from a trap. "My children go to school and no one pays any attention. One English child told Lorna she had heard one of my records and thought it was all right. I have found I can go shopping and be absolutely unnoticed like anyone else." Judy Garland is 38 now. She was a star at 14. What happened over those years? "For just about 16 years it was keep your weight down to 98 pounds. Don't eat this. Don't eat that. I grew up in Minnesota where we ate beans and bread. Take a pill so you can go to work. Take a pill to go to sleep so you can get up to go to work again. Well when I was fired and had no money I moved into the biggest hotel in Los Angeles the waiters brought the food in like a procession: I had no money and they looked at me queerly so I went to New York and did the same thing." This was the girl who was the biggest money maker in the film industry at one time. How much did she really make? "I have no idea. I never did. Most of us don't." After the break with the studio magnates Judy says the salvation of her sanity came from husband Sid. "The doctors told me I was finished" she said "Washed up. You know when that sank in, I was almost glad. Then I could say to myself, 'That's over' and relax for the first time. Now I had to back away and count up how much I owed, and how much money I needed. My husband did that for me. If Hollywood wants me to make a movie" Judy said "I'll work on it with pleasure. But I will go there only for that and will not live there"[2]

At this same time, producer Stanley Kramer was putting together a movie version of a *Playhouse 90* television broadcast about the Nuremberg trials. Plans were to expand the narrative and fill the roles with top

Returning to the Concert Stage—*Judgment at Nuremberg* (1961)

level actors. At first, Garland wasn't considered. Kramer wanted Julie Christie to play the role of Irene Hoffman. Then this item appeared from columnist Lee Merriman:

> Julie Harris was all signed by Stanley Kramer for a part in *Judgment at Nuremberg*. Then Judy Garland's agent got to Kramer and convinced him that Judy's name on theater marquees would sell more tickets than Julie's. Kramer paid Julie off and hired Judy. It's no reflection on Julie's talents. It's just a case of that old hard-and-fast Hollywood formula—the Star System.[3]

Judgment at Nuremberg

Directed and produced by Stanley Kramer
Screenplay by Abby Mann (based on his story)
Cinematography by Ernest Laszlo
Film editing by Frederic Knudtson
Cast: Spencer Tracy, Burt Lancaster, Richard Widmark, Marlene Dietrich, Maximilian Schell, Judy Garland, Montgomery Clift, William Shatner, Werner Klemperer, Kenneth MacKenna, Torben Meyer, Joseph Bernard, Alan Baxter, Edward Binns, Virginia Christine, Otto Waldis, Karl Swenson, Martin Brandt, Ray Teal, John Wengraf, Ben Wright, Howard Caine, Olga Fabian, Paul Busch, Sheila Bromley, Victor Buono, Jana Taylor, Oscar Beregi, Jr., Jack Berle, John Clarke, Bess Flowers, Sam Bagley, Paul Bradley, Brad Brown, Herman Hack, Lorna Hanson, Harold Miller, Hans Moebus, Ed Nelson, William H. O'Brien, Paul Power, Walter Raney, Norbert Schiller, Rudy Solari, Norman Stevans, Hal Taggart, Mitchell Rhein, Bert Stevens, Jack Stoney, Clark Ross, Waclaw Rekwart, Sam Harris, Tony Regan, Shep Houghton, Walter Raney, Reed Howes, George Nardelli, William Maeder, Ralph Moratz, Bobby Gilbert, Frank Baker, Sayre Dearing, Joseph Crehan, Brandon Beach, and Dick Cherney
Released December 19, 1961
179 minutes
Roxlom Films Inc, for United Artists
Black and White

Judgment at Nuremberg isn't a Judy Garland film, per se, but it is also not a mere cameo like she had done in *Ziegfeld Follies* or *Words and*

The Films of Judy Garland

Music. It was a serious role, and Garland was among several other noted stars who were playing parts. But she was by no means overshadowed. In fact, her performance was one of the film's true standouts.

Judy Garland's role in *Judgment at Nuremberg* was to play Irene Hoffman, a middle-aged German hausfrau who had once been forced to testify for the Nazis and took a prison sentence before she'd lie on the stand. Her testimony was misrepresented in court, resulting in a beloved father figure, Mr. Feldenstein, being put to death, essentially because he was Jewish. Garland expected to have to crash diet and get in shape for the role, and was pleased when Stanley Kramer assured her that this was not necessary for the character. She definitely does not look glamorous in this movie, and her more dowdy appearance suits this character well. It is very unlike any of her other film roles. This was the first movie since *The Clock* where Garland did not sing.

Irene Hoffman, now Irene Wallner, is asked to testify at the Nuremberg trials by Colonel Tad Lawson (Richard Widmark), an American

Judy Garland was nominated for both an Oscar and a Golden Globe for her performance in *Judgment at Nuremberg*.

Returning to the Concert Stage—*Judgment at Nuremberg* (1961)

who believes the Nazis should not get away with the atrocities they committed. Irene is reluctant, and her husband, Hugo Wallner (Howard Caine), adamantly refuses, but Colonel Lawson persuades Irene to testify. When she is on the stand, her answers to Lawson's questioning are shaky but determined, wanting to reveal the facts. But the cross-examination by Nazi Hans Rolfe (Maximilian Schell) loudly interrogates Irene in the same manner that she received in the past. She insists that her relationship with Feldenstein was filial at the most, and nothing went beyond that. Rolfe forces Irene to admit that she kissed the man, sat on his lap, and knew that it was against the law to be even this friendly with someone Jewish—a law Irene chose to ignore because of the man's genuine kindness.

> HANS ROLFE: Remember, it was disclosed at the tribunal that Mr. Feldenstein bought you things. Candy and cigarettes?
> IRENE HOFFMAN: Yes.
> HANS ROLFE: Did you sit on his lap?
> IRENE HOFFMAN: Yes. But there was nothing wrong or ugly about it.
> HANS ROLFE (LOUDLY ENUNCIATING EACH WORD): Did—you—sit—on—his—lap?
> IRENE HOFFMAN: Yes, but
> HANS ROLFE: You sat on his lap! What else did you do?
> IRENE HOFFMAN: *Why* do you not let me speak the truth?
> HANS ROLFE: That's what we want, Mrs. Wallner. The truth. The truth!

Judy Garland, with limited screen time, delivers a performance that resonates throughout the film, trembling with both fear and anger, exhibiting her mounting frustration, and ultimately bursting into tears. She suffers through the reliving of having to defend Feldenstein's kind benevolence while Hans Rolfe tries to reconstruct her narrative as if there was a sexual relationship, be it consensual or rape.

Despite her long experience and immense talent, Garland had trouble playing this role. The reason, quite uncharacteristic of her, was that she was too happy. Everything was going exceptionally well for her, with sold out concerts, hit records, a new agent (Freddie Fields, whose ideas appeared very promising), and the sort of settled existence for which she had always longed. In fact, when Garland first appeared on the set to start work, the crew gave her a standing ovation. But, she was a professional and knew that she could effectively call up the emotions necessary to exhibit Irene's terror, anger, frustration, and sadness. She did so brilliantly.

Garland filmed her scenes for *Judgment at Nuremberg* from March 8–19, 1961. A month later, she would perform at a sold-out Carnegie Hall concert, when Stanley Kramer called her back to the set for some retakes. For the first time during this project, Garland panicked. She worried that such an emotional role would affect her voice for the concert. She nearly had a breakdown. Stanley Kramer intervened. He reminded her that this was no longer the studio system, and that he was an independent producer. All she had to do was let him know and the retake dates could be changed. This relieved Garland greatly. She performed the Carnegie Hall concert on April 23, 1961, and it was the most successful one of her entire career. Some even called it the greatest night in show business history. The concert was recorded, and the resulting double album spent 13 weeks at the top of the Billboard charts. She would return to Carnegie Hall for another sold out triumph on May 21.

When *Judgment at Nuremberg* was released, it netted an Oscar nomination for Judy Garland, despite it being a small part of a big movie that was filled with top-level actors. She did not win (she lost to Rita Moreno for *West Side Story*), but was quite pleased with the nomination, and was interested when Stanley Kramer inquired about another project he was planning with the same screenwriter, and one of the film's stars, Burt Lancaster. But first, Garland had some other projects to consider.

The first time Judy Garland saw *Judgment at Nuremberg* was when she attended a screening at the time of her Hollywood Bowl Concert in September 1961. Then in October, while she was touring on the east coast, Capitol Records hired her to record two singles for release as 45 rpm records. She recorded "Comes Once in a Lifetime" and "Sweet Danger" at Capitol's New York studios with arranger/conductor Mort Lindsey.

Also in October 1961, Judy Garland agreed to provide the voice of Mewsette for animator Chuck Jones' feature length project *Gay Purr-ee*. The songwriters were Harold Arlen and E.Y. Harburg, who had scored *The Wizard of Oz* over 20 years earlier. Expecting the film to be a big hit, Garland agreed to be paid $50,000 and ten percent of the gross, a big contract for such a project.

Gay Purr-ee

Directed by Abe Levitow
Screenplay by Dorothy and Chuck Jones

Returning to the Concert Stage—*Gay Purr-ee* (1962)

Produced by Chuck Jones
Film editing by Earl Bennett and Sam Horta
Animation Department:
    Steve Clark, sequence director; Hal Ambro, animator; Arthur Davis, animator; Phil Duncan, animator; Ken Harris, animator; Volus Jones, animator; Don Lusk, animator; Fred Madison, animator; Ray Patterson, animator; Grant Simmons, animator; Hank Smith, animator; Irven Spence, animator; Harvey Toombs, animator; Ben Washam, animator; Paul Allen, animator; Bob Bransford, animator; Bob Carlson, animator; Ed Friedman, animator; Bill Justice, animator; Abe Levitow, animator; Milt Neil, animator; Claude Smith, animator; Don Towsley, animator; Judge Whitaker, animator; Bob Inman, color stylist; Dick Kelsey, color stylist; Phill Norman, color stylist; Don Peters, color stylist; Gloria Wood, color stylist
Songs:
    All music was composed by Harold Arlen, and the lyrics were written by E.Y. Harburg.
    "Gay Purr-ee Overture"
    "Mewsette"
    "Take My Hand, Paree"
    "Roses Red, Violets Blue"
    "The Money Cat"
    "The Horses Won't Talk"
    "Bubbles"
    "Little Drops of Rain"
    "Paris Is a Lonely Town"
    "The Mewsette Finale"
Cast (Voices): Judy Garland, Robert Goulet, Red Buttons, Paul Frees, Hermione Gingold, Mel Blanc, Morey Amsterdam, Joan Gardner, and Julie Bennett
Released October 24, 1962
85 minutes
Produced UPA for Warner Brothers release
Technicolor

With Sid Luft exploring other business ventures, Garland's new agent Freddie Fields was asked to straighten out the situation with CBS. This resulted in the settling of her contract disputes and two more specials. The first aired on February 25, 1962, and featured Frank Sinatra and Dean Martin as Garland's guests. Another special featured her old friend Phil Silvers and new friend Robert Goulet, her co-star in a

The Films of Judy Garland

Technicolor musical in which she and Goulet lent their voices to a couple of animated cats.

The success of *Judgment at Nuremberg* resulted in Judy Garland securing a few contracts for subsequent movies, including another with *Nuremberg* director Stanley Kramer, penned by that film's screenwriter, Abbe Lane, and featuring that film's star, Burt Lancaster, as Garland's co-star. She also was signed to do another big musical drama. But before that, Judy Garland agreed to lend her voice to an animated cartoon feature planned by UPA studios.

United Productions of America (UPA) was an animation studio that began when several Disney animators left the company during a strike in 1941. One of them was John Hubley, who revolutionized animation by believing it did not have to be so realistic as had been presented, and could be more limited. UPA connected with Columbia Pictures studio, which resulted in such classic cartoons as the Oscar winning *Gerald McBoing Boing* and the Mr. Magoo series, which itself netted two Oscars. UPA produced only two feature length animated movies—*1001 Arabian Nights*, which featured Mr. Magoo, and *Gay Purr-ee*, which was written by Chuck Jones and his wife Dorothy and directed by Abe Levitow.

By the early 1960s, Chuck Jones was a well-established producer, director, writer, and animator. Working at the infamous Termite Terrace, where the great Merrie Melodies and Looney Tunes were made for Warner Brothers, Jones did cartoons featuring Bugs Bunny, Porky Pig, Daffy Duck, Road Runner, and Pepe LePew. Out of eight Academy Award nominations, Jones won three. Some consider Chuck Jones to be the finest animation filmmaker of them all.

Abe Levitow had worked at Warner Brothers since the 1940s and had been a credited animator since the 1950s, working on cartoons directed by Chuck Jones. He directed a handful of Bugs Bunny cartoons before moving over to UPA at the end of the 1950s to work on the Mister Magoo and Dick Tracy cartoons the company was then making for television. Abe Levitow also directed the feature length TV cartoon *Mr. Magoo's Christmas Carol*, which was a big hit on the small screen. He had also worked on UPA's previous feature-length theatrical cartoon, *1001 Arabian Nights*.

Gay Purr-ee features Judy Garland as the voice of Mewsette, a cat that lives on a dreary farm in 19th-century France. She longs for the beauty of Paris, so she runs away and hops onto a train that takes her to the city, leaving behind Jaune Tom (voice of Robert Goulet), a male cat

Returning to the Concert Stage—*Gay Purr-ee* (1962)

***Gay Purr-ee* was an animated feature that was expected to be more successful.**

that adores her, and his little friend Robespierre (voice of Red Buttons). She meets con artist Meowrice (Paul Frees). He introduces her to the chic Madame Henrietta Rubens-Chatte (Hermione Gingold) that has plans to teach her manners and sophistication. Mewsette believes she is being groomed for Paris society, when in fact Meowrice plans to turn her into a profitable mail-order bride for a fat, unattractive cat waiting in America. Meanwhile, Jaune Tom and Robespierre have followed Mewsette to Paris. Meowrice happens to see that Jaune Tom is an expert mouser. He gets Jaune Tom and Robespierre drunk and sells them as mousers to a ship bound for Alaska. Through a series of circumstances, Mewsette realizes Meowrice's ulterior motives and runs away, while Jaune Tom and Robespierre strike gold in Alaska and can afford a trip back to Paris. Mewsette, alone and lonely, attempts to jump off a bridge, but is captured by Meowrice and his "henchcats" and taken by train to a ship that will take her to America. Madame Rubens-Chatte, angry that Meowrice paid for her services with a worthless check, helps Jaune Tom and Robespierre get to the train to rescue Mewsette, resulting in a fight scene. Jaune Tom and Mewsette end the film enjoying the beauty of Paris together.

Gay Purr-ee is a very colorful film with a few artistic highlights. One is a sequence where Meowrice is taking Mewsette around the sites of Paris, as artist renditions of the Eiffel Tower, the Champs-Élysées, and the Moulin Rouge (called "Mewlon Rouge" in the movie) are presented. Another is when Meowrice commissions paintings of Mewsette by Claude Monet, Henri de Toulouse-Lautrec, Georges Seurat, Henri Rousseau, Amedeo Modigliani, Vincent van Gogh, Edgar Degas, Auguste Renoir, Paul Cézanne, Paul Gauguin, and Pablo Picasso, with the animation artists presenting renditions of these styles. There are also comic highlights. Meowrice has a violent run-in with a bulldog voiced by Mel Blanc, and the final fight on the boxcar of a moving train has some fun cartoon slapstick.

The soundtrack is, overall, unremarkable, but the musical number "The Money Cat" featuring Meowrice and his henchcats is fun and presented with interesting animation artistry, while the song "Paris Is a Lonely Town," sung by Mewsette, is another highlight. Judy Garland would later indicate the song "Little Drops of Rain" was a favorite of hers and would sometimes add it to her concert set list.

It was unusual back then for top stars to voice cartoons, even feature length ones (a practice that has since become quite common). But in 1962, it was remarkable for a superstar like Judy Garland to voice a cartoon character. Chuck Jones hoped to get Elvis Presley to voice Jaune Tom, and while Presley was intrigued with the prospect of singing with Judy Garland, it didn't seem like the right project for him while he was making movies like *Girls Girls Girls* and *Kid Galahad*. And, of course, his manager, Colonel Tom Parker, nixed the idea immediately because the film would have Presley off screen and part of an ensemble. Robert Goulet was a star on Broadway in *Camelot* and had been scoring in his TV appearances, so he was chosen for the voiceover.

With noted performers, including top level cartoon voice veterans like Paul Frees and Mel Blanc, and an artistically colorful and impressive visual presentation, it seemed *Gay Purr-ee* couldn't miss. Sadly, it was a box office flop. According to one theater owner who wrote to the trade magazine *BoxOffice:*

> Too artistic and highbrow for small towns, definitely for the high class set. Might do as part of a double bill, but its chances are pretty slim unless you get the kids in. Had many walkouts and hisses.[4]

Returning to the Concert Stage—*A Child Is Waiting* (1963)

While younger moviegoers would enjoy the characters and comic highlights, the story that included mail-order brides, drinking to the point of getting drunk, even a suicide attempt, was a bit edgy for their tastes, especially as far back as the early 60s. The artist renditions are impressive for a knowledgeable adult, but would be lost on children. And the songs are more adult-oriented, easy-listening fare.

Gay Purr-ee also caused a problem for Chuck Jones. When UPA made the production available for distribution, it was picked up by Warner Brothers, with whom Jones had an exclusive contract. When they discovered he had "moonlighted" and produced a film for another production company, they fired him. Jones went over to MGM and began working on a new series of Tom and Jerry cartoons. Abe Levitow joined him. At MGM, Jones won another Oscar for *The Dot and the Line: A Romance in Lower Mathematics*, and also produced the classic animated TV version of Dr. Seuss' *How the Grinch Stole Christmas* with Boris Karloff doing the narration.

Because a top star voicing a cartoon feature was not common, the fact that *Gay Purr-ee* flopped did not affect Judy Garland's film career. The entire enterprise was dismissed as an aberration and was quickly forgotten. Garland then went on to film the other movies she was contracted to do.

A Child Is Waiting

Directed by John Cassavetes
Screenplay by Abby Mann
Produced by Stanley Kramer
Film editing by Gene Fowler, Jr., and Robert C. Jones
Cast: Burt Lancaster, Judy Garland, Gena Rowlands, Steven Hill, Paul Stewart, Gloria McGehee, Lawrence Tierney, Bruce Richey, John Marley, Bill Mumy, Elizabeth Wilson, Jim Backus, John Cassavetes, June Walker, James Rawley, Juanita Moore, Bruce Cocoran, Fred Draper, Mario Gallo, Barbara Pepper, Butch Patrick, Michael Stevens, Noam Pitlik, and Marilyn Clark
Released January 11, 1963
102 minutes
Stanley Kramer Productions for United Artists Release
Black and White

The Films of Judy Garland

Stanley Kramer's plan to re-team Burt Lancaster and Judy Garland from *Judgment at Nuremberg* in a new project was announced in Louella Parsons' column over a year before the film's release:

> Obviously, Stanley Kramer is very pleased with Judy Garland and Burt Lancaster in *Judgment at Nuremberg*, for he has both of them on a contract to co-star in *A Child Is Waiting*. Judy will do this before she films *The Lonely Stage*,[5] and Burt will face the cameras for Kramer before he stars in *The Leopard*, and, best of all news, is that it will be made right in good old Hollywood at the Revue Studios. Another member of the *Judgment at Nuremberg* group, Abby Mann, who wrote *Nuremberg*, will produce *A Child Is Waiting*. The story deals with mentally ill children, and Burt plays a doctor, with Judy as a nurse.[6]

Parsons was incorrect in naming Abby Mann as the producer; Mann wrote the screenplay and Kramer produced. The director was to be British-born Jack Clayton, but he dropped out due to a scheduling conflict, so John Cassavetes took over direction at the request of Abby Mann.

Judy Garland had been enjoying a successful career renaissance that gave her confidence about her work. Agent Freddie Fields had straightened out her TV contract, and the success of the subsequent specials resulted in CBS offering her $24 million to star in her own musical-variety series, which was to debut in September 1963. However, by the time she filmed *A Child Is Waiting*, Garland was dealing with a tumultuous marriage once again, as her relationship with husband Sid Luft was falling apart. They would separate in 1963 and eventually divorce in 1965. Stanley Kramer believed that a stable work environment would be helpful to Garland, and believed she was up to doing the role. Garland had been involved in child charities in the past, so a film about mentally challenged kids and the altruistic nurse who tries to help them seemed perfect for her. Burt Lancaster recalled, "Judy was drinking a great deal, and it was a big effort to get herself together and get in shape to work.... I had to kind of nurse her along with it. And because of her mental condition at the time, she wasn't terribly involved with the part."[7]

Judy Garland plays Julliard graduate Jean Hansen, who is hired by the Crawthorne State Mental Hospital but disagrees with the methods utilized by its director, Dr. Matthew Clark (Burt Lancaster). Jean connects with Reuben (Bruch Richey), a 12-year-old patient, and believes his issues could be helped if he were to reconnect with the parents who abandoned him. Dr. Clark disagrees, but Jean sends for the boy's mother. She sides with the doctor, but the boy sees her leaving the hospital and

Returning to the Concert Stage—*A Child Is Waiting* (1963)

Ad for the film *A Child is Waiting*.

chases her car. Reuben is deeply hurt and flees the hospital. While Dr. Clark retrieves the boy, Jean plans to resign. Dr. Clark asks her to stay and continue working on a Thanksgiving pageant planned for the parents to attend. Reuben's father shows up for the pageant, intending to take him out of the hospital and enroll him elsewhere, but after he sees his son recite a poem in the show, he realizes the hospital has had a positive influence on Reuben and leaves him in Jean's care.

Stanley Kramer stated that his intention was "to throw a spotlight on a dark-ages type of social thinking which has tried to relegate the subject of retardation to a place under the rocks."[8] For authenticity, he had several mentally challenged kids in the film as extras. Burt Lancaster was interviewed on the set about this and stated, "We have to ad-lib around the periphery of a scene and I have to attune and adjust myself to the unexpected things they do. But they are much better than child actors for the parts. They have certain gestures that are characteristic, very difficult for even an experienced actor."[9]

Despite the problems in her private life, and Burt Lancaster's claim that she had trouble connecting with the work as a result, Judy Garland turned in a magnificent performance in only the third non-musical dramatic role in her career. However, she had trouble responding to John Cassavetes' unusual approach to direction, and she wasn't alone. Burt Lancaster had the same response, as did Stanley Kramer. Editor Gene Fowler recalled, "It was a fight of technique. Stanley is a more traditional picture-maker, and Cassavetes was, I guess, called Nouvelle Vague. He was trying some things, which frankly I disagreed with, and I thought he was hurting the picture by blunting the so-called message with technique."[10] Cassavetes was fired during the editing process and subsequently disowned the movie.

Unfortunately, in the 1960s, only the critics were impressed with a movie like *A Child Is Waiting*. They praised the film and the performances. But moviegoers were not interested in this subject matter at the time, and although it has gained in popularity and respect over the years, *A Child Is Waiting* was not of interest upon its initial release. It didn't even make back half its production costs at the box office.

A Child Is Waiting walks a line between being overly sentimental and a little edgier, so in tone and style it feels a bit off (perhaps due to that clash between Cassavetes and Kramer). It's an important movie, but perhaps a bit ahead of its time. Garland is wonderful, but so are Gena Rowlands and Steven Hill as Reuben's parents, especially the

Returning to the Concert Stage—*I Could Go on Singing* (1963)

latter. They convincingly relate the heartbreak regarding their complicated situation. Richey is also excellent as Reuben.

However, *A Child Is Waiting* can still be considered a positive for Judy Garland the actress. Once again, she showed that her innate skill as an actress was so formidable that she was able to turn her personal pain into her performance. All of Jean Hansen's passions, frustrations, and disappointments were understood by Garland and she very capably made the character her own. *A Child Is Waiting* features some of her career-best work as an actress.

Not long after production ended on *A Child Is Waiting*, Garland went into her next intended movie project. The plan to make a film out of Robert Dozier's story *The Lonely Stage* got underway. This British-American production was retitled *I Could Go on Singing* so that audiences would know that Garland would be singing in a film for the first time since *A Star Is Born*, save for her voiceover performance in *Gay Purr-ee*. It would be her final motion picture.

I Could Go on Singing

Directed by Ronald Neame
Screenplay by Mayo Simon (from the teleplay *The Lonely Stage* by
    Robert Dozier for *Studio One*)
Produced by Saul Chaplin, Stuart Millar, and Lawrence Turman
Cinematography by Arthur Ibbetson
Film editing by John Shirley
Songs:
    "I Am the Monarch of the Sea"; Lyrics and music by Gilbert and
        Sullivan
    "Hello Bluebird"; Lyrics and music by Cliff Friend
    "It Never Was You"; Lyrics and music by Kurt Weill and Maxwell
        Anderson
    "By Myself"; Lyrics and music by Arthur Schwartz and Howard
        Dietz
    "I Could Go on Singing"; Lyrics and music by Harold Arlen and
        E.Y. Harburg
Cast: Judy Garland, Dirk Bogarde, Jack Klugman, Aline MacMa-
    hon, Gregory Phillips, Russell Waters, Pauline Jameson, Jeremy

The Films of Judy Garland

Burnham, Eric Woodburn, Robert Rietti, Gerald Sim, David Lee, Leon Cortez, Al Paul, Laurie Heath, Frazer Hines, Jonathan Morris, Tony Robinson, Jack Arrow, Hyma Beckley, Jack Berg, Ernest Blyth, Daniel Brown, Ted Carroll, Victor Croxford, Mabel Etherington, Chick Fowles, Muriel Greenslade, Patrick Halpin, Aidan Harrington, Victor Harrington, Kathleen Heath, Billy John Juba Kennerly, Jay McGrath, Colin McKenzie, Paul Phillips, Pat Ryan, George Spence, Emile Stemmler, Phillip Stewart, Pearl Waters, Fred Wood, Sheila Aza, Joyce Everson, Otto Friese, Pat Lewis, Lorna Luft, Fred Machon, Louis Matto, Richard Neller, and Paddy Smith
Released March 7, 1963 (World Premiere, London), March 20, 1963 (Miami, Florida), May 15, 1963 (New York, New York)
99 minutes
Barbican Films for United Artists Release
Technicolor

I Could Go on Singing will always be most significant for being Judy Garland's final film. The trajectory of her movie career, from *Pigskin Parade* to this point, was one of diverse ideas and emotions, and it culminates here. *I Could Go on Singing* is not the cinematic masterpiece that Judy Garland deserved to have conclude her movie career. But it is much better than its negative reputation. Based on *The Lonely Stage*, a 1958 television drama that starred Mary Astor, the story was expanded from its original one-hour length to feature film running time, and included several big song numbers. Only one actor, Jack Klugman, was retained from the TV production.

Judy Garland plays Jenny Bowman, a concert singer who is often on tour. While performing in London, Jenny makes the decision to visit David Donne (Dirk Bogarde), with whom she had an affair years ago that resulted in the birth of a son, Matt (Gregory Phillips). David is now a successful surgeon, and was recently widowed. It is he who has raised Matt, who was told he was adopted. Jenny and David agreed to never tell Matt the truth, but Jenny wants to meet him at least once, so David takes her to his boarding school. Jenny and Matt get along well, sharing a natural subconscious parental connection that Matt doesn't realize. After spending a happy day together, Jenny invites David and Matt to her Palladium concert that night. David is unable to make it because of work in Rome. With David in Rome, Jenny spends the next several days with Matt, even getting her manager (Jack Klugman) to call the boarding school to cover for his absences. But word soon reaches David that Matt has not been attending. He returns, and Matt

Returning to the Concert Stage—*I Could Go on Singing* (1963)

overhears their argument, discovering they are his biological parents. Jenny wants Matt to accompany her on her tour, while David insists he remain in London for school. Matt refuses to go with Jenny, but the two realize they can now have an honest relationship. A downtrodden Jenny goes out drinking and injures her foot. At the clinic, she requests that David treat her. She tells him, quite passionately, that she wants to quit singing because she feels overwhelmed by it all. David convinces her to continue and promises to remain with her until he believes she's okay. As she does her closing number for an audience that has been waiting over an hour, Jenny looks to see David waiting in the wings throughout the song. When she is about midway through, she looks again and sees he is no longer there.

Viewing *I Could Go on Singing* can cause a lot of conflicting reactions. It isn't a particularly good movie overall, especially to culminate Judy Garland's great screen career, but it also features some of her finest work as an actress. The scene in the hospital where Jenny explodes with emotion is a particular highlight, especially if, as has been stated in previous studies, it was Garland herself extemporaneously supplying her character's dialogue.

Garland had not read the entire script until she arrived in London to begin shooting. She only knew it was a dramatic story with music about a performer who triumphs at the London Palladium late in her career, just as Garland herself had done. She didn't like the script at all, and refused to start work. Dirk Bogarde had the same misgivings and discussed with Garland the possibility of rewriting the dialogue in their scenes to make it more acceptable. She agreed, but it was mostly Bogarde who did any rewriting.

Garland was treated very well on the set by the cast and crew. Screenwriter Mayo Simon stated, "The theory was that if we all just loved and admired her enough, everything would be okay. It turned out that there wasn't that much love in the world."[11] However, Judy Garland was very challenging to work with throughout production. Despite her happiness and success only a few years ago, Garland was now in a much more fragile state. For a few days she'd be working comfortably and happily, then she'd disappear for several days and return angry and belligerent. But, somehow, through all of this, her innate talent emerges on screen. Her song numbers are powerful, and the complex acting role that calls for her character to go from cheerful to weary to despondent was handled expertly.

There are elements to Jenny that really do connect well with Judy

Judy Garland stars opposite Dirk Bogarde in her final movie, *I Could Go on Singing*.

Garland—the dry sarcasm that hides both weariness and emotional pain, the lackadaisical attitude that is still no match for her talent once she hits the stage, and the aforementioned hospital scene, when Jenny bares her soul, real-life Garland seemed to connect with the situation and embellished the written dialogue with her own feelings beyond her performance. According to director Ronald Neame:

> This scene was about a four-minute, five-minute scene, which I intended to break up into a medium shot and a close two-shot, and then individuals. We rehearsed it, and I said fine, let's now shoot it. Now, some extraordinary piece of magic happened. It was a very dramatic scene, where the Judy character says "I'm never going back to the theater again. I'm not going to go there and put myself up there, and why should I sing when I don't want to sing." So, a big argument. And suddenly, on the first shot, which was supposed to finish a quarter of the way through, suddenly, I realized that this was real life. Judy had become the real Judy. It was no longer acting, and it was absolutely wonderful. She bared her heart to Dirk. Whilst we were shooting, I thought, "My God, what am I going to do?" Because this was a one-time thing. So I did this [waved him forward] to the character pushing the camera, to get him to

Returning to the Concert Stage—*I Could Go on Singing* (1963)

go in closer, which he did, he crept in closer. And Dirk Bogarde, being a brilliant actor and a very good film person, he realized what was happening, and he moved in closer to her. So they were right close, and so I was able to come in closer. And we went right through the whole six minutes, I suppose, of the scene, and everybody on the set was in tears when we said cut. I said that's it. We'll never ever get that again. So it is all in one shot.[12]

This scene is not only the highlight of *I Could Go on Singing*, it is one of Judy Garland's best acted scenes in all of her pictures. Her dialogue truly resonates:

I can't be spread so thin, I'm just one person. I don't want to be rolled out like a pastry so everybody can get a nice big bite of me. I'm just me. I belong to myself. I can do whatever I damn well please with myself and nobody can ask any questions. You think you can make me sing? Do you think you can—do you think George can make me sing? Or Ida? You can get me there, sure, but can you make me sing? I sing for myself. I sing when I want to, whenever I want to, just for me. I sing for my own pleasure. Whenever I want—do you understand that?

When she is finally convinced to go to the Palladium where the audience has been waiting over an hour, she is confronted by her long suffering manager, who says:

It's an hour past curtain. You'll be forty-five minutes getting dressed. Do you think they're gonna wait for you? There are twenty-five hundred people out there who paid money to see Jenny Bowman. But you're gonna let them down. Now, that may not mean anything to you anymore, but I still have a certain reverence for audiences. They mean a great deal to me. But if they still do mean something to you, then I'm gonna find it very difficult to forgive you. And if they don't mean anything to you anymore, then … then I am genuinely and profoundly sorry for you, Jenny.

It can be argued that Jack Klugman's performance in this scene matches the brilliance of Dirk Bogarde, and of Judy Garland, making the final scene of *I Could Go on Singing* that much more powerful.

When the despondent Jenny reaches the stage, it gives us a glimpse of how well she handled her audience, and how much they loved her—an accurate parallel to Judy Garland herself. She jokes about being late, points out her expensive fur, insisting "I shot it!" and asks for the curtain to open, stating, "they probably fell asleep back there." When she sings the title song as the movie concludes, it is the usual Judy Garland showstopper.

The story for *I Could Go on Singing* may be rather routine and underwhelming, but Garland consistently elevates the material. In the scenes where she is performing at the Palladium, it really does feel like we are watching the magic of her stage shows, from her singing to her wisecracks at the audience. You also really feel the emotional weight behind all the songs when she sings. It is interesting to see her in a musical film like this that was a version of her concert career, as opposed to a traditional musical like the ones that made her famous.

Another beautiful, heartbreaking scene that comes before the hospital scene is the one where Jenny is on the phone with Matt, when he is telling her that he chooses to keep living with his father as opposed to going off with her. The camera stays on Garland as opposed to cutting back and forth between Jenny and Matt, and you can really see her devastation gradually unfold.

Critics were mixed in their reaction to *I Could Go on Singing*, naturally not realizing it would be Judy Garland's final movie. *Variety* stated:

> *I Could Go on Singing* is pretty weighty cargo. Although handsomely mounted and endowed with Judy Garland, one of the great stylists of her generation, the production is constructed on a frail and fuzzy story foundation. A soulful performance is etched by Garland who gives more than she gets from the script. She also belts over four numbers as only she can belt them, yet the impact of a live Garland stage performance is not duplicated on the screen on this occasion. The camera tends to remain in too tight. Bogarde seems somewhat ill-at-ease in his role, employing two basic expressions—pain and a kind of confused "what am I doing here?" or "somebody must be kidding."[13]

While the consistently stodgy Bosley Crowther in the *New York Times* wrote:

> Considering what Judy Garland has done in movies over the years and how many of her fans still love her, no matter what she does, it is sad to have to say the little lady is not at the top of her form in her new film, "I Could Go on Singing," which came to the Astor and other theaters yesterday. The face is a little puffy, the figure a trifle plump and the old pipes are not so melodious and vibrant as they used to be. Nor does she have the timing and that wonderfully frank, ingenuous air she had.... Furthermore, she overacts badly when she sings out her heartbreak in the song, "I'll Go My Way by Myself," tears glistening in her eyes.... I can't even give very high marks to Harold Arlen's and E.Y. Harburg's title song, which Miss Garland belts out for the finish. No, it's rather sad, all around.[14]

Despite all of the difficulties with Garland during the shooting, *I Could Go on Singing* was completed on budget and in only twelve weeks from May to July 1962. Judy Garland did all the post-production looping

Returning to the Concert Stage—*I Could Go on Singing* (1963)

necessary and one last close-up shot that was needed to insert during a scene. After that, director Neame told her that was it, they were done. Garland looked to the crew and stated, "you'll miss me." And they did. A subsequent actress they worked with was far more troublesome and had none of the magnificent talent that Garland had. Judy Garland was always able to obliterate any on-set challenges by truly rising to the occasion when the cameras rolled. And she certainly did that in what was to be her final film.

The Final Years

Judy Garland sued Sid Luft for divorce in 1963, and began an affair with actor Glenn Ford, which lasted for about six months and, according to accounts by biographer Gerald Clarke and Glenn Ford's son, Peter, was one of the more stable relationships for both. It reportedly ended when Garland wanted to marry and Ford did not.

Garland's network TV program, *The Judy Garland Show*, was nominated for four Emmy Awards, but only lasted one season, due to being telecast opposite the popular *Bonanza*.

In August 1963, Judy Garland joined Josephine Baker, Sidney Poitier, Lena Horne, Paul Newman, Rita Moreno, and Sammy Davis, Jr., for the March on Washington for Jobs and Freedom, a demonstration organized to advocate for the civil and economic rights of African Americans. A month later, Garland joined daughter Liza, Carolyn Jones, June Allyson, and Allyson's daughter Pam Powell for a press conference to protest the bombing of the 16th Street Baptist Church in Birmingham, Alabama, in which four young African American girls perished.

Judy Garland returned to the Palladium in 1964 for a triumphant performance that also included daughter Liza Minnelli, but a tour of Sydney, Australia, that same year was not a success. While the shows had to be scheduled for the stadium because none of the concert halls were big enough for the demand for tickets, Garland's erratic behavior (showing up late, performing poorly) caused the audiences to heckle her and force her to leave the stage.

In 1965, Garland married her tour manager Mark Herron but separated five months later, each accusing the other of violent behavior. Garland separated from agent Freddie Fields in 1966, believing he mismanaged her funds, and that Fields' partner David Begelman had embezzled a lot of her money.[1] As she owed half a million dollars, the IRS put liens on Garland's home in Brentwood, her record royalties, and any other income. Garland sold her home at less than its value to help with her debts.

The Final Years

In 1967, Garland signed on to appear in the film *Valley of the Dolls*, but her behavior, and reported mistreatment by an impatient director, resulted in her being fired from the film. She returned to the stage at the New York Palace Theater that same year for 75 percent of the profits, but most of her payment was seized by the IRS. In poor health at the end of the 1960s, Judy Garland performed in London and, for the final time, in Copenhagen. In March 1969, she married nightclub manager Mickey Deans in London.

On June 22, 1969, Judy Garland was found dead due to an overdose of drugs. She had attempted suicide often over the years, always being rescued. Sadly, this time there was no rescue. Garland had only $40,000 and many debts, despite being one of the biggest and greatest stars of

Judy Garland died in June 1969.

The Films of Judy Garland

the 20th century. Frank Sinatra stepped in and helped pay the debts she left behind.

When Judy Garland died, newspapers across the country printed tributes to the actress, and many stars offered their sincere condolences. But perhaps the most genuine, and moving, tribute showed up in the Letters section of the Racine, Wisconsin, newspaper the *Journal Times*. It stated:

> When I was 13, I used to go to the movies three times a week. It was cheaper then. I never missed a Judy Garland picture. I sat through the movies three times. When I left it was not me anymore, I was Judy Garland. The Venetian Theater had a long staircase leading up to the balcony and I would go up there and walk down very slowly. No one noticed me, but I pretended they did. I dreamed of meeting Judy Garland someday, but I didn't get to do that. I wanted her to know how much I loved her. Judy Garland gave herself, a little bit to each one of us. Maybe that's why she died at 47. She had given all she had.[2]

The letter was simply signed "Reflective," but it beautifully indicates just how much the fans loved Judy Garland in her time.

The personal and professional challenges that Judy Garland faced were strong enough to end her life far too early. But they were no match for her talent. The work that Garland left behind, from films, television, and recordings, will continue her magnificent legacy.

The films of Judy Garland represent another aspect of her enormous talent. From the cute yearning of adolescent Betsy Booth, to the adventure of Dorothy Gale, the spirited determination of Esther Smith, the suffering of Vicki Lester, and the powerful impact of Irene Hoffman, Judy Garland's acting career was diverse and versatile. Her films present not only the legacy of a great musical star, but of a fine actress who met the challenge of every role she played.

Chapter Notes

The Early Years

Pigskin Parade

1. Gerold Frank, *Judy*, New York: Harper and Row, 1975.

Thoroughbreds Don't Cry

2. "What The Picture Did For Me," *Motion Picture Herald*, June 4, 1938.
3. Sophie Tucker, *Some of These Days*, New York: Doubleday, 1945.

Everybody Sing

4. *Everybody Sing* review, *Los Angeles Evening Citizen News*, February 10, 1938.

Love Finds Andy Hardy

5. "Young Cinema Star Gets Broken Ribs in Auto Crash," *Appeal-Democrat*, May 26, 1938.
6. *Love Finds Andy Hardy* review, *Los Angeles Times*, July 14, 1938.

Listen, Darling

7. Gerold Frank, *Judy*, New York: Harper and Row, 1975.
8. *Listen, Darling* review, *Box Office*, December 3, 1938.

The Wizard of Oz

9. "Goldwyn To Sell *Wizard of Oz*," *Los Angeles Times*, February 18, 1938.
10. Louella Parsons Column, International News Syndicate, February 23, 1938.
11. Often erroneously credited to actor Spencer Bell.
12. James L. Neibaur, *The W.C. Fields Films*, Jefferson, NC: McFarland, 2017.
13. *The Making of the Wizard Of Oz*, Documentary, 1979.
14. *Wizard of Oz* review, *Movies and the People Who Make Them*, 1939.

Babes in Arms

15. James L. Neibaur, *The Essential Mickey Rooney*, Lanham: Rowman and Littlefield, 2016.
16. Hugh Fordin, *The World of Entertainment: Hollywood's Greatest Musicals*, New York: Doubleday, 1975.
17. James L. Neibaur, *The Essential Mickey Rooney*, Lanham: Rowman and Littlefield, 2016.
18. Variety Staff, "*Babes in Arms*," *Variety*, September 20, 1939.
19. "The Exhibitor Has His Say: *Babes in Arms*," *Box Office*, January 1940.

Andy Hardy Meets Debutante

20. James L. Neibaur, *The Essential Mickey Rooney*, Lanham: Rowman and Littlefield, 2016.
21. "Andy Hardy Meets Debutante," *Variety*, July 3, 1940.

Strike Up the Band

22. "Young Movie Star in Upper Bracket at $2000 in Hollywood," United Press syndicated article, September 29, 1940.
23. "Police Guard Judy Garland After Telephoned Threat," *Los Angeles Times*, March 8, 1940.
24. Willie is played by Larry Nunn, whose daughter Terri Nunn was the lead singer of the group Berlin that had a hit

Chapter Notes

record with "Take My Breath Away" in 1986.

25. James L. Neibaur, *The Essential Mickey Rooney*, Lanham: Rowman & Littlefield, 2016.

26. Hugh Fordin, *The World of Entertainment: Hollywood's Greatest Musicals*, New York: Doubleday, 1975.

27. Frank Nugent, "Mickey Rooney and Judy Garland 'Strike Up the Band,' at the Capitol, Opening a Bag of Tricks," *New York Times*, September 30, 1940.

28. "Strike Up the Band," *Variety*, September 18, 1940.

Little Nellie Kelly

29. Frank Miller, "Little Nellie Kelly," TCM.com.

30. Hedda Hopper Column, *Los Angeles Times*, November 17, 1940.

31. *Little Nellie Kelly* review, *Film Daily*, November 15, 1940.

32. *Little Nellie Kelly* review, *Los Angeles Times*, November 16, 1940.

33. "What the Picture Did For Me," *Motion Picture Herald*, January 25, 1941.

34. Fan Forum, *Screenland*, November 1940.

Ziegfeld Girl

35. Louella Parsons Column, International News Service, April 15, 1938.

36. Sidney Skolksy Column, *Los Angeles Evening Citizen News*, June 13, 1938.

37. Louella Parsons Column, International News Service, June 27, 1939.

38. "Ann Miller possibility for *Ziegfeld Girl*," *Los Angeles Times*, July 10, 1940.

39. "Dramatic Story Announced for *Ziegfeld Girl*," *Los Angeles Times*, July 30, 1940.

40. "Modern Ziegfeld Girls Will Be Sought," *Los Angeles Times*, July 1, 1940.

Babes on Broadway

41. James L. Neibaur, *The Essential Mickey Rooney*, Lanham, MD: Rowman and Littlefield, 2016.

42. Thomas Pryor, "Babes on Broadway," *New York Times*, January 1, 1942.

For Me and My Gal

43. Louella Parsons Column, International News Syndicate, February 26, 1942.

44. Hugh Fordin, *The World of Entertainment: Hollywood's Greatest Musicals*, New York: Doubleday, 1975.

45. *For Me and My Gal* review, *Los Angeles Daily News*, November 26, 1942.

Presenting Lily Mars

46. *Presenting Lily Mars* review, *Los Angeles Citizen Evening News*, July 2, 1943.

Girl Crazy

47. Mickey Rooney interview with the author, August 2001.

48. James Agee, "Girl Crazy," *Time*, December 27, 1943.

49. "Girl Crazy," *Variety*, December 4, 1943.

Meet Me in St. Louis

50. John Sturdevant, "Hollywood Headache," *San Francisco Examiner*, August 6, 1944.

The Clock

51. Hugh Fordin, *The World of Entertainment: Hollywood's Greatest Musicals*, New York: Doubleday, 1975.

52. Hugh Fordin, *The World of Entertainment: Hollywood's Greatest Musicals*, New York: Doubleday, 1975.

53. Joe Morella and Eddie Epstein, *The Films of Judy Garland*, New York: Citadel Press, 1969.

The Harvey Girls

54. *Harvey Girls* review, *Film Daily*, January 3, 1946.

55. *Harvey Girls* review, *New York Times*, January 25, 1946.

The Pirate

56. Hedda Hopper Column, *Los Angeles Times*, January 19, 1947.

Chapter Notes

57. Gerold Frank, *Judy*, New York: Harper and Row, 1975.
58. *The Pirate* review, *Los Angeles Times*, June 26, 1948.

Easter Parade

59. Gerold Frank, *Judy*, New York: Harper and Row, 1975.
60. Hugh Fordin, *The World of Entertainment: Hollywood's Greatest Musicals*, New York: Doubleday, 1975.
61. "Irving Berlin Plugging 'Easter' Film," *Los Angeles Evening Citizen News*, July 23, 1948.
62. "*Easter Parade* is a Musical that Has Everything," *San Francisco Examiner*, July 15, 1948.
63. Rooney would later appear in films released or distributed by MGM, but he was no longer under contract with the studio.

Summer Stock

64. "Summer Stock," The Judy Room, www.thejudyroom.com.

Back on Stage

1. Judy Garland biography, Wikipedia.

A Star Is Born

2. Gerold Frank, *Judy*, New York: Harper and Row, 1975.
3. Ibid.
4. Ronald Haver, "A Star Is Born Again," *American Film Magazine*, July–August 1983.

Returning to Concert Stage

1. Jerry Lewis interview with the author, October 1992.
2. Tom Reedy, "Judy Garland Enjoys Freedom," London Newspaper Syndicate, January 22, 1961.
3. Lee Merriman, Editor's Diary, *Pasadena Independent*, March 23, 1961.

Gay Purr-ee

4. "Gay Purr-ee," *BoxOffice*, November 25, 1963.

A Child in Waiting

5. The working title for Judy Garland's next film, *A Child Is Waiting*.
6. Louella Parsons column, International Press Syndicate, October 14, 1961.
7. Gary Fishgall, *Against Type: The Biography of Burt Lancaster*, New York: Scribner, 1995.
8. Gary Fishgall, *Against Type: The Biography of Burt Lancaster*, New York: Scribner, 1995.
9. Ibid.
10. Gary Fishgall, *Against Type: The Biography of Burt Lancaster*, New York: Scribner, 1995.

I Could Go On Singing

11. Gerald Clarke, *Get Happy: The Life of Judy Garland*, New York: Delta, 2001.
12. "I Could Go On Singing," thejudyroom.com.
13. *I Could Go on Singing* review, *Variety*, May 18, 1963.
14. *I Could Go on Singing* review, *New York Times*, May 16, 1963.

The Final Years

1. Begelman would also be involved in an embezzlement and forgery scandal involving Columbia Pictures and actor Cliff Robertson. Begelman would later commit suicide.
2. Letters to the Editor, *Journal Times*, June 27, 1969.

Bibliography

Books

Behlmer, Rudy. *Memo from David O. Selznick*. New York: Grove, 1972.

Clarke, Gerald. *Get Happy: The Life of Judy Garland*. New York: Delta, 2001.

Fishgall, Gary. *Against Type: The Biography of Burt Lancaster*. New York: Scribner, 1995.

Fordin, Hugh. *The World of Entertainment: Hollywood's Greatest Musicals*. New York: Doubleday, 1975.

Frank, Gerold. *Judy*. New York: Harper and Row, 1975.

Hay, Peter. *MGM: When the Lion Roars*. Atlanta: Turner Publishing, 1991.

Loy, Myrna. *Being and Becoming*. New York: Knopf, 1987.

McGilligan, Patrick. *George Cukor: A Double Life*. New York: HarperCollins, 1992.

Morella, Joe, and Eddie Epstein. *The Films of Judy Garland*. New York: Citadel Press, 1969.

Neibaur, James L. *The Essential Mickey Rooney*. Lanham, MD: Rowman and Littlefield, 2016.

_____. *The W.C. Fields Films*. Jefferson, NC: McFarland, 2017.

Thompson, Frank, and John Gallagher. *Nothing Sacred: The Cinema of William Wellman*. Asheville, NC: Men with Wings Press, 2018.

Tucker, Sophie. *Some of These Days*. New York: Doubleday, 1945.

Wayne, Jane Ellen. *Clark Gable: Portrait of a Misfit*. New York: St. Martin's Press, 1993.

Young, Gwenda. *Clarence Brown*. Lexington: University Press of Kentucky, 2018.

Articles and Reviews

Agee, James. "Girl Crazy." *Time*, December 27, 1943.

"Andy Hardy Meets a Debutante." *Variety*, July 3, 1940.

Babes in Arms review. *Variety*, September 20, 1939.

Everybody Sing review. *Los Angeles Evening Citizen News*, February 10, 1938.

"Exhibitor Has His Say." *Box Office*, January 1940, November 25, 1963.

Girl Crazy review. *Variety*, December 4, 1943.

"Goldwyn To Sell Wizard of Oz." *Los Angeles Times*, February 18, 1938.

Haver, Ronald. "A Star is Born Again." *American Film Magazine*, July–August, 1983.

Hedda Hopper Column. *Los Angeles Times*, November 17, 1940, January 19, 1947.

I Could Go On Singing review. *New York Times*. May 16, 1963.

I Could Go On Singing review. *Variety*, May 18, 1963.

Listen Darling review. *Box Office*, December 3, 1938.

Little Nellie Kelly review. *Film Daily*, November 15, 1940.

Little Nellie Kelly review. *Los Angeles Times*, November 16, 1940.

Louella Parsons Column. International News Syndicate, February 23, 1938, April 15, 1938, June 27, 1939, February 26, 1942, October 14, 1961.

Love Finds Andy Hardy review. *Los Angeles Times*, July 14, 1938.

Merriman, Lee. Editor's Diary. *Pasadena Independent*, March 23, 1961.

"Modern Ziegfeld Girls Will Be Sought." *Los Angeles Times*, July 1, 1940.

Nugent, Frank. "Strike Up the Band." *New York Times*, September 30, 1940.

"Police Guard Judy Garland After Telephoned Threat." *Los Angeles Times*, March 8, 1940.

Bibliography

Sidney Skolksy column. *Los Angeles Evening Citizen News*, June 13, 1938.
Strike Up the Band review. *Variety*, September 18, 1940.
"What the Picture Did for Me." *Motion Picture Herald*, January 25, 1941.
Wizard of Oz review. *Movies and the People Who Make Them*, 1939.
"Young Cinema Star Gets Broken Ribs in Auto Crash." *Appeal-Democrat*, May 26, 1938.
"Young Movie Star in Upper Bracket at $2000 in Hollywood." United Press syndicated article, September 29, 1940.

Online Sources

The Judy Room. thejudyroom.com.
TCM.com
Internet Movie Database
Wikipedia

Documentaries

The Making of The Wizard of Oz. Documentary (1979). Dir. Bruce Franchini.

Interviews

Jerry Lewis with the author, September 1992.
Mickey Rooney with the author, August 2001.

Index

Adler, Stella 85
The Adventures of Tom Sawyer 68
Alexander's Ragtime Band 130
Allyson, June 99, 138, 148, 182
Alton, Robert 128
Ames, Leon 103, 106
Anchors Aweigh 126, 133
Andy Hardy Meets Debutante 54, 55–58, 63
Annie Get Your Gun 142, 143
Arlen, Harold 41, 166, 167, 180
Astaire, Fred 78, 116, 129, 131, 132, 133, 134, 135, 136, 138, 147
Astor, Mary 31, 32, 104, 105, 176
Autry, Gene 133

Babes in Arms 46, 48–54, 55, 57, 58, 61, 63, 67, 80
Babes on Broadway 79–83
The Bachelor and the Bobby-Soxer 133
Bainter, Fay 91
Baker, Josephine 182
The Barkleys of Broadway 138
Bartholomew, Freddie 19, 30, 41, 33
Baum, Frank 26, 34, 36, 37, 38, 39, 41
Beckett, Scotty 31
Benson, Sally 101, 106, 107
Berkeley, Busby 53, 62, 81, 87, 88, 98, 99, 142
Berlin, Irving 130, 13, 132, 135, 136
Berman, Pandro S. 76
The Big Review 3
The Big Wheel 144
Bogarde, Dirk 176, 177, 178, 179, 180
Bolger, Ray 39, 40, 44, 46, 47, 122
Boys Town 30, 55, 68
Bracken, Eddie 144, 147, 148
Brando, Marlon 158
Brecher, Irving 107
Bremer, Lucille 104
Brice, Fanny 23, 25
Broadway Melody of 1936 15
Broadway Melody of 1938 10, 13, 14, 15–18, 21, 24, 67

Bruce, Virginia 71
Burke, Billie 23
Burton, Richard 158
Buttons, Red 168
Byington, Spring 91, 139

Cantinflas 162
Capra, Frank 133
Carmichael, Hoagy 3
Carroll, Joan 104, 105
Carson, Jack 169
Carver, Lynne 33
Casablanca 139
Cassavetes, John 172, 174
Chaplin, Charlie 70
Charisse, Cyd 122, 133
A Child Is Waiting 171–175
The Clock 108, 109–115, 116, 117, 123, 125, 164
Cohan, George M. 65, 68, 83
Cooper, Jackie 19, 54, 75
Country Girl 160
Cover Girl 144
Crain, Jeanne 106
Crawford, Joan 71
Crosby, Bing 120, 121, 150, 151, 152, 153
Cukor, George 41, 42, 43, 155, 158, 159, 160
Curtis, Billy 44

Dailey, Dan 49, 75
David Copperfield 19
Davis, Sammy, Jr. 182
Deans, Mickey 183
DeHaven, Gloria 138, 144, 145
The Devil Is a Sissy 19
Donen, Stanley 138, 148
Dorsey, Tommy 120
Dot and the Line: A Romance in Lower Mathematics 171
Downs, Johnny 8
Drake, Tom 104
Dramatic School 70
Duke, Patty 106

191

Index

Durbin, Deanna 5, 6, 7, 9, 10, 11, 12, 14, 21, 25, 91
Dwan, Dorothy 38

Earles, Harry 44
Easter Parade 129–136, 137, 138
Ebsen, Buddy 15, 16, 17, 39
Eggerth, Martha 92
Erwin, Stuart 7, 9
Eshbaugh, Ted 41, 47
Every Sunday 5, 6, 10, 11, 12
Everybody Sing 22–26
Eyes of the Night 111

Fabares, Shelley 107
Fields, Freddie 165, 167, 172, 182
Finklehoffe, Fred 80, 101, 107
For Me and My Gal 83–89, 93, 126
Ford, Glenn 133, 182
Foster, Preston 119, 122
Four Star Playhouse 161
Frawley, William 67
Freed, Arthur 13, 16, 41, 49, 50, 62, 65, 68, 81, 85, 87, 93, 98, 101, 103, 104, 106, 110, 111, 118, 122, 127, 130, 131, 132, 133, 136, 138, 140, 142, 144, 148

Gable, Clark 10, 13, 14, 15, 17, 19, 43, 57, 75
Gallagher, Ed 73
Gallico, Paul 111
Gallico, Paula 111
Gardner, Ava 82
Garson, Greer 116
Gay Purr-ee 166–171, 175
Gerald McBoing Boing 168
Gershwin, George 54, 60, 96
Gershwin, Ira 96
Gilmore, Will 33
Gingold, Hermione 169
Girl Crazy 93, 95–99, 142
Goddard, Paulette 70
Going My Way 106
Gone with the Wind 43, 106
Good News 60
Goodrich, Albert 128
Goulet, Robert 167, 168, 170
Grable, Betty 8
Grant, Cary 158
Green, Mitzi 49
Gumm, Dorothy Virginia 4
Gumm, Ethel 2, 33, 59, 156
Gumm, Frank 3, 5, 33
Gumm, Mary Jane 4

Hackett, Albert 128
Hale, Alan 31
Haley, Jack 7, 9, 34, 39, 40, 45
Hamilton, Margaret 41, 42, 45, 50, 58, 62, 65
Harburg, E.Y. "Yip" 41, 81 166, 180
Hardy, Oliver 38
Harlow, Jean 9
The Harvey Girls 116–122, 123
Haver, Ronald 160
Heflin, Van 91, 92, 93
Herron, Mark 182
High Noon 111
Hill, Steven 174
Hodiak, John 118, 120, 122, 123
Holden, Fay 22
A Holiday in Storyland 3
The Hollywood Review of 1929 16
Holm, Celeste 107
Horne, Lena 182
Horton, Edward Everett 75
How the Grinch Stole Christmas 171
Hubley, John 168
Hunter, Tab 107
Hutton, Betty 142, 143

I Could Go On Singing 175–182
I Love Lucy 67
In the Good Old Summertime 137–142

Johnny Eager 91
Johnson, Van 138, 139, 140
Jolson, Al 161
Jones, Allan 23, 24
Jones, Carolyn 182
Jones, Chuck 166, 168, 170, 171
Judgment at Nuremberg 1, 163–166, 168, 172

Kanin, Garson 125
Karloff, Boris 171
Keaton, Buster 138, 139, 140, 141
Kelly, Gene 85, 86, 87, 88, 89, 116, 126, 127, 129, 131, 132, 133, 138, 144, 145, 146, 147. 148
Kelly, Grace 160
Kelly, Patsy 7, 9
Kelly, Paul 75
Kid Glove Killer 111
Kidnapped 19
Kilbride, Percy 147
The Kissing Bandit 138
Klugman, Jack 176, 179
Kohler, Fred, Jr. 7

Index

Jessel, George 3
Judge, Arlene 8

Kern, Jerome 123
Kramer, Stanley 162, 163, 164, 166, 168, 172, 174

Lady in the Dark 153
Lahr, Bert 39, 40, 45, 46
Lamarr, Hedy 71, 72, 73, 74, 76
Lambert, Jack 122
Lancaster, Burt 166, 168, 172, 174
Lansbury, Angela 118, 119, 121, 123
Lawford, Peter 60, 133, 134, 135, 136
LeRoy, Mervyn 41, 49, 50, 71
Levitow, Abe 168, 171
Lewis, Jerry 161
Life Begins for Andy Hardy 76–79
Listen, Darling 30–33, 37
Little Nellie Kelly 63, 64–69
Locke, Tammy 107
Lockhart, June 104
Lombard, Carole 3
Love Finds Andy Hardy 26–30
Loy, Myrna 10, 46, 107
Luft, Joseph 161
Luft, Lorna 3, 45, 153, 156, 162
Luft, Sid 149, 152, 153, 155, 156, 158, 161, 167, 172, 182

Main, Marjorie 144, 145, 147
Marren, Jerry 44
Martin and Lewis 67–68
Marx Brothers 133
Mason, James 157, 158, 159
Mayer, Louis B. 3, 6, 9, 32, 49, 60, 65, 66, 82, 88, 93, 101, 133, 142, 144
McGuire, William Anthony 71
McHenry, Curtis 38
McPhail, Douglas 65, 66, 67, 68
Meet Me in St. Louis 23, 31, 101–108, 111, 159
The Merry Macs 120
Miller, Ann 133
Minnelli, Liza 45, 62, 123, 124, 125, 141, 182
Minnelli, Vincente 62, 101, 104, 105, 106, 107, 111, 113, 116, 123, 124, 125, 126, 127, 129, 131, 142, 149
Mr. Magoo's Christmas Carol 168
Modern Times 70
Moreno, Rita 182
Morgan, Frank 40, 46, 73
Murphy, George 15, 16, 17, 65, 67, 68, 85, 88, 89, 91

Neame, Ronald 178–179, 181
Newman, Paul 182
Nicholas Brothers 49
Nunn, Larry 62

O'Brien, Margaret 103, 104, 105, 106, 108
O'Brien, Virginia 121
Olivier, Lawrence 158
On the Town 138

Pal Joey 132
Parker, Cecilia 22
Pasternak, Joe 7, 9, 11, 12, 90, 91, 93, 137, 138, 139, 140, 143, 144
Pepe 162
The Phil Silvers Show 147
The Philadelphia Story 75
Phillips, Greg 176
Pidgeon, Walter 31, 32, 106
Pigskin Parade 5–10, 12, 14, 16, 176
The Pirate 123–128, 130, 135
Pitts, ZaSu 9
Playhouse 90 162
Poitier, Sidney 182
Porter, Cole 78, 127, 128
Powell, Eleanor 15, 71, 82, 85
Powell, Pam 182
Power, Tyrone 158
Preisser, June 50, 60, 61
Presenting Lily Mars 71, 72, 89–95, 99.
Presley, Elvis 68, 152, 170

Quicksand 144
Quine, Richard 86

Raabe, Meinhart 44
Raye, Martha 63
Richey, Bruch 172, 176
Rodgers and Hart 53, 136
Rooney, Mickey 18, 19, 20, 21, 22, 25, 26, 27, 28, 30, 37, 46, 48, 49, 50, 51, 52, 53, 54, 55, 56, 57, 58, 60, 61, 62, 63, 67, 76, 78, 79, 80, 81, 82, 83, 85, 93, 94, 97, 98, 99, 136, 137, 144
Rose, David 63, 79, 82, 95
Rowlands, Gena 174
Rutherford, Ann 22, 26

Sakall, S.Z. 139
Selznick, David O. 85, 155
Semon, Larry 37, 38, 39, 47, 67
The Seventh Cross 111
Shaw, Artie 39, 54, 57, 63
Shaw, Reta 107

Index

Shean, Al 73
Sheldon, Sidney 135
The Shop Around the Corner 137, 138
Silvers, Phil 39, 54, 59, 91, 128, 144, 147, 167
Simon, Mayo 177
Sinatra, Frank 126, 133, 135, 138, 152
Since You Went Away 113
Sinclair, Ronald 19, 20
Skelton, Red 116, 135
Slezak, Walter 127
Smith, C. Aubrey 19
Snow White and the Seven Dwarfs 36, 37, 41, 45
Sondergaard, Gale 41
Stack, Robert 125
A Star Is Born 1, 23, 148, 153–160, 161, 175
Stevenson, Robert Louis 19
Stewart, James 71, 74, 75
Stone, Lewis 22
Strike Up the Band 54, 58, 59–63, 64
Sullavan, Margaret 71
Sully, Robert 104
Summer Stock 142–149
Sundberg, Clinton 139

Tarkington, Booth 91
Taurog, Norman 67, 68, 93, 98, 99
Taylor, Robert 75, 91
Temple, Shirley 17, 36, 37, 81
Thorpe, Richard 41, 155
Thousands Cheer 93
Three Smart Girls 5, 7, 9, 11, 12, 14
Three Stooges 133

Todd, Thelma 9
Tracy, Spencer 75, 111, 125
Tucker, Sophie 15, 16, 19, 20, 21
Turner, Lana 26, 28, 54, 57, 71, 72, 73, 84, 76, 91, 116, 117
Twentieth Century 3

Valley of the Dolls 183
Van Dyke, Marcia 139

Walker, Robert 111, 112, 113, 115, 123
Walters, Charles 93, 129, 131, 132, 133, 142, 144, 148
Waters, John 45
The Wedding of Jack and Jill 3
Weidler, Virginia 80, 81
What! No Beer? 139
What Price Hollywood? 155
Wheeler, Bert 96
Whiteman, Paul 61, 63
Wills, Chill 123
Winninger, Charles 52, 65, 67, 68, 73
The Wizard of Oz 1, 23, 26, 30, 31, 33–48
Woolsey, Robert 96
Words and Music 137

The Young in Heart 70
Yule, Joe 94

Ziegfeld Follies 116
Ziegfeld Girl 67, 69–76
Zinnemann, Fred 111

www.ingramcontent.com/pod-product-compliance
Ingram Content Group UK Ltd.
Pitfield, Milton Keynes, MK11 3LW, UK
UKHW042010140426
5217IPUK00015B/1086